OXFORD WORLD'S CLASSICS

THE NEW OXFORD SHAKESPEARE

General Editors for The New Oxford Shakespeare:
Gary Taylor, John Jowett, Terri Bourus, Gabriel Egan
General Editor for Oxford World's Classics: Emma Smith

The New Oxford Shakespeare offers authoritative editions of Shakespeare's works combining cutting-edge textual scholarship with editorial material from leading scholars in the field. Derived from the landmark *The New Oxford Shakespeare Complete Works: Modern Critical Edition*, these Oxford World's Classics editions have been designed with today's reader, student, and playgoer in mind, offering fresh interpretations of Shakespeare's plays and poems alongside comprehensive critical apparatus. New introductions provide context and criticism drawn from the latest research in the field; notes on the text detail the editorial decisions made and alternative possibilities; and the bibliography points readers to more research on specific plays, topics, and on Shakespeare Studies as a whole.

HAILEY BACHRACH is a Leverhulme Early Career Fellow at Roehampton University, where her fellowship project, Shakespeare and Consent, explores depictions of consent to sex and marriage on the early modern stage, and how contemporary artists grapple with the issues these raise. She completed her PhD at King's College London in collaboration with the Globe, including working as a rehearsal room researcher in the 2019 history plays cycle. She is the author of *Staging Female Characters in Shakespeare's English History Plays* (2023).

ANNA PRUITT is the managing editor of Giving USA at the Lilly Family School of Philanthropy at Indiana University. She is an associate editor of *The New Oxford Shakespeare*.

T0300699

THE NEW OXFORD SHAKESPEARE

OXFORD WORLD'S CLASSICS

WILLIAM SHAKESPEARE

Richard II

With an Introduction by
HAILEY BACHRACH

Text edited by
ANNA PRUITT

OXFORD
UNIVERSITY PRESS

Great Clarendon Street, Oxford, OX2 6DP,
United Kingdom

Oxford University Press is a department of the University of Oxford.
It furthers the University's objective of excellence in research, scholarship,
and education by publishing worldwide. Oxford is a registered trade mark of
Oxford University Press in the UK and in certain other countries

Published in the United States of America by Oxford University Press
198 Madison Avenue, New York, NY 10016, United States of America

British Library Cataloguing in Publication Data

Data available

Library of Congress Control Number: 2024935238

ISBN 978-0-19-888196-4

Printed and bound in the UK by
Clays Ltd, Elcograf S.p.A.

PREFACE

Why read a new Shakespeare edition? Why read this one?

The answer to this question is paradoxical. In part it draws on Shakespeare's perennial interest or timelessness, and in part on the opposite, timeliness: the changing understanding of how his texts might operate in their own world and ours.

Shakespeare's perennial interest is a familiar enough concept. Since Ben Jonson's prescient comment about his friend and rival as 'not of an age but for all time' in the prefatory poem to the first collected edition of the plays in 1623, we have been used to recognizing Shakespeare's genius as a version of longevity. If, as Italo Calvino suggested, a classic is 'a book which has never exhausted all it has to say to its readers', Shakespeare is indefatigable.

But part of this timelessness is actually a serial topicality. Shakespeare is timely because his works continue to speak to issues of identity, politics, and culture in new ways. 'Cross-dressing' characters read differently as ideas around binary gender shift; the green world of the comedies strikes a different note in a climate emergency; mobs on stage echo with fears about the energies of populism. The plays often capture a significant moment in the consolidation of certain cultural fictions—about racial difference, for instance, or about the place of the individual in a larger historical frame. The new introductions to this edition are attentive to the ways Shakespeare is meaningful right now, as well as across time.

Alongside these new interpretative resonances are, literally, new texts. The history of editing Shakespeare's works has been shaped by assumptions about him. Was he an inspired poet who really disdained his popular audiences and their demands, as earlier editors used to suggest? Or was he passionate about theatre as a genre in which the author is only one agent of meaning, and in which bringing the work to life involves a collaborative team including actors, musicians, stagehands, and audiences? The inspired poet model tends to produce tidy texts emphasizing linguistic fluency and singular authorship; the theatrical model is more interested in the idea that Shakespeare worked with other writers and that his works were themselves dynamic scripts rather than static literary monuments. According to this latter logic, then, all versions of a play in print are provisional, of their time. And so too are the ones printed in this series.

Emma Smith

CONTENTS

GENERAL EDITORS' PREFACE
TO *THE NEW OXFORD SHAKESPEARE*

The Oxford World's Classics Shakespeare is based upon the texts and commentaries of *The New Oxford Shakespeare: Complete Works*. That edition was produced by an international multigenerational team, using new research tools and methods to investigate systematically several interrelated historical and textual questions. What did Shakespeare write? When did he write it? Which of his works were written in collaboration with other playwrights? Which of his posthumously published texts contain later revisions or additions (by himself or others)? How did the evolving infrastructure and routines of the early modern multimedia entertainment industry influence what Shakespeare wrote and how it was performed? How did the technology of early modern printing and the economics of early modern bookselling influence the texts that survive? Were specific texts censored? What do his words mean? How were they pronounced in his lifetime? How should they be spelled for modern readers? How should his sentences be punctuated for modern readers and actors? How can, or should, prose be distinguished from verse? Can we recover the original music for the songs in his plays?

The New Oxford Shakespeare offers readers more forms of his writing than any other edition. Uniquely, it contains two different printed editions of the *Complete Works*. The *Critical Reference Edition* (in original spelling and punctuation) includes textual and bibliographical introductions with comprehensive textual notes; the works are arranged in the order in which the texts were first edited, from the 1592 printing of *Arden of Faversham* to the 1727 printing of *Double Falsehood*, Lewis Theobald's adaptation of Shakespeare and Fletcher's *The History of Cardenio*. In contrast, the *Modern Critical Edition* (in modernized spelling and punctuation) introduces each work with a curated international bricolage of verbal and visual responses by scholars, critics, actors, and artists over the centuries; its commentaries focus on semantic and performance interpretation; the works are arranged in the order in which they seem to have been written, beginning with *The Two Gentlemen of Verona* (1587?) and ending with *The Two Noble Kinsmen* (1613–14). An *Authorship Companion* surveys the external and internal evidence for what Shakespeare wrote and when he wrote it. The *New Oxford Shakespeare Online* combines and links both versions of the *Complete Works* with the *Companion*, supplementing them all with linked digital images of the original documents. Finally, the *Complete Alternative Versions* brings together additional texts of those plays and poems that exist in more than one early but significantly different incarnation, ranging from the 1594 printing of *The First Part of the Contention of the Two Famous Houses of York and Lancaster* to the 1623 printing of *The Tragedy of King Lear*; again, each text in the *Critical Reference Edition* is also presented in a *Modern Critical Edition*, and all are incorporated into Oxford Scholarly Editions Online, alongside the *Complete Works*.

Every edition of Shakespeare seeks to preserve and restore the complex, radiant energies of the artistic objects he created more than four centuries ago. But in the *New Oxford Shakespeare*, each of Shakespeare's surviving works is edited from a uniquely systematic and comprehensive perspective. Moreover, unlike most editions of Shakespeare, the *New Oxford Shakespeare* is not a reprint of any previous edition. It is based on direct re-examination of the surviving original documents. But no early modern text is entirely error-free, and different copies of the same edition contain variants introduced during printing. There is no evidence that Shakespeare himself proofread any of the texts of his work printed in his own lifetime. Shakespeare's editors try to do the proofreading that Shakespeare did not.

Even when early printers accurately reproduced the manuscripts they had purchased, those manuscripts themselves may have differed, intentionally or unconsciously, from what Shakespeare originally wrote. Handwritten manuscripts, like hand-printed editions, all contain unintended mistakes. In addition, texts could not be published or performed in early modern England unless they had been read, approved, and licensed by politically appointed officials, who could remove or alter material they considered objectionable. Punishments for criticizing the monarchy (treason) or the state religion (blasphemy and treason) were severe; allusions to important persons, incitements to public disorder, or words too explicitly sexual were also likely to be censored. Just what constituted 'objectionable' varied with time and the censor's own preferences. Demonstrably, some early texts of

Shakespeare's plays were censored on political and religious grounds. And some modern editions censor Shakespeare, too, by either preferring censored texts or refusing to explain his sexual meanings. We gloss delicate sexual innuendoes delicately, but when Shakespeare used a pointedly crude or vulgar expression, our commentary supplies a crude modern equivalent.

The Oxford World's Classics Shakespeare, like the *Modern Critical Edition*, seeks to make Shakespeare as accessible as possible for contemporary readers. Almost everyone first encounters Shakespeare by reading a modernized text or hearing a modernized performance (just as every modern reader of the Bible begins with an edited text translated from several ancient languages). Our texts apply the principles for scholarly modernization of spelling developed by Sir Stanley Wells in 1979, which have been widely praised and adopted. When the original spellings are ambiguous, we record both interpretations of the word in the commentary notes. We also modernize the text by using markers (diacritics) over certain letters to clarify the rhythms of the verse. We take for granted the modern elided form of the past participle (where a word like 'charged' is a monosyllable) but add an accent to call attention to the now-obsolete two-syllable pronunciation often used by Shakespeare and his contemporaries, as in 'Shall stand sore chargèd for the wasteful vengeance' (*Henry V* 1.2.283). For the same reason, we use a diaeresis to indicate the obsolete disyllabic pronunciation of 'ion', as in 'Such beastly shameless transformatïon' (*Henry IV, Part I* 1.1.44), or 'ean', as in 'A peaceful progress to the ocëan' (*King John* 2.1.340). Likewise, when modern usage stresses a different syllable, we indicate the obsolete pronunciation with an accent, as in 'As other of such vinegar aspèct' (*Merchant of Venice* 1.1.54).

Gary Taylor, John Jowett,
Terri Bourus, and Gabriel Egan

INTRODUCTION

In a prison cell, a king sits alone—more or less. He is a crownless king, so perhaps he is not a king at all. And he is not quite alone. After all, he has his imagination, and that can 'beget | A generation of still-breeding thoughts; | And these same thoughts people this little world' (5.5.7–9) of his confinement.

In a prison cell, a king sits alone—but he isn't alone, because he has an audience to speak to. Crowned as an infant, King Richard has spent his entire life in front of spectators, a court waiting breathlessly for him to live up to the reputations of his father and grandfather, the first a glorious warrior who died too young and the second a decisive and prosperous king who secured his legacy with seven sons.

Sitting down to watch or picking up a copy of one of Shakespeare's history plays often seems like a fraught prospect. What do you need to know about those seven sons, about Richard's reign, about everything that came before and after the small slice of English history you're going to see? It's usually an experience propped up by apparatus: editors and artists hurrying to supply the missing knowledge without which the play supposedly simply cannot stand. *Richard II* is perhaps considered particularly in need of these external supports, famous both for its dense offstage historical backstory and for its association with Queen Elizabeth I and key events of her reign.

But *Richard II* is also Shakespeare's most lyrical history play—the only one written entirely in verse—and perhaps his most human. Rather than building to a climactic battle, a clash of armies and ideals, the play grows narrower and narrower in scope, shrinking down—like the world of its titular character—until its penultimate scene presents us with a man alone in a prison cell, who invites us to step into his mind and live in a world populated only by his thoughts.

This makes *Richard II* one of Shakespeare's most readable plays. Even only in writing, the characters brim with personality that the play's stodgy reputation conceals. The story speaks for itself. This Introduction aims to present *Richard II* as a rich piece of theatre, not simply an episode in a long and complex historical serial, and to combat the rigidity of the history play's reputation—the charts, the tables, the dates, the family trees—and imagine all of the other things

Richard II is and can be: 'in one person many people' (5.5.31) within the play that bears that capaciously imaginative king's name.

The Play in History (and the History Play)

Imagine you are a playgoer in 1595, when *Richard II* likely had its first performances. You might occupy any of the startling range of social positions that attended the public playhouses in early modern England, to say nothing of private performances in royal courts and wealthy homes: aristocrat, merchant, apprentice, tourist. Perhaps you sell food and drink to playgoers, or seize the chance to pick the pockets of an attentive—and thus inattentive—audience. Maybe you know a smattering of Latin and Greek from your grammar school education, or you're a wealthy collector of books and own a copy of one of the chronicle histories of England, huge tomes that brought together narratives of varying accuracy about the country's past. Maybe you are a veteran playgoer and have seen the anonymous play *Thomas of Woodstock*, which also depicts the reign of King Richard II. Down at the tavern, maybe you heard someone sing a ballad like the mid-sixteenth century 'The Cronycle of all the Kyngs', a rhymed list set to music of the regnal dates and key features of the reigns of the English kings.[1] While that particular song far predates *Richard II*, it's an example of how an average English person might have learned a bit of history: through publicly sung songs set to popular tunes, whose lyric sheets were sold so that people could have a copy of their favourite ballads to read, or even perform, at home.

If someone happened to learn about King Richard through 'The Cronycle', they would find that 'In [his] time was peace great plenty [. . .] And at Langley was buried first, so stood the case | And after to Westminster his body carried was'.[2] This could hardly be more different from the rapacious and violent reign depicted in *Thomas of Woodstock*, which some scholars present as a sort of prequel to *Richard II*, a basis for playgoer knowledge about the unfortunate

[1] 'The Cronycle of all the Kyngs' (EBBA 32098), Huntington Library—Britwell, HEH18279, https://ebba.english.ucsb.edu/ballad/32098.
[2] Ibid.

king, but newer evidence suggests may not have been written until afterwards, and may never have been performed.[3]

But even if *Woodstock* should not be considered a 'prequel', the contrast in content between it and 'The Cronycle' is a reminder that when we imagine ourselves as an 'average' playgoer or reader, there is no real way to know what that actually meant in terms of historical knowledge—something an experienced playwright like Shakespeare would have known very well. By this point, Shakespeare had been writing professionally for the Lord Chamberlain's Men for around five years, and had experimented with a wide range of genres, from comedy (including *A Midsummer Night's Dream*) to tragedy (including *Romeo and Juliet*) to history plays (the *Henry VI* plays and *Richard III*). It's certainly possible that Shakespeare was writing with an educated, aristocratic audience in mind and didn't much care how the public playhouses received the story, but the fact remains that the majority of people who would see *Richard II* would enter the playhouse with unique and varied understandings of the history they were about to watch: as literary critic Benjamin Griffin writes, 'allusions to the playgoers who got their history from the plays, [. . .] span nearly the whole social spectrum. The popular literary arts—plays, ballads, and pamphlets—formed, for the illiterate and the learned alike, a segmented but continuous patchwork History-of-England in the mind.'[4] Every playgoer's mental patchwork would be just a little different in colour and tone and content, the scraps pieced together by their experiences not quite the same.

History plays were therefore seen in the period not just as reinforcement of, or reflection on, what playgoers already knew, but as active and educational. They come up repeatedly in defences of the public playhouses, always framed as a tool for inspiration in the present, not just for depicting the past. Admittedly, these writers had an agenda—to defend a still-nascent art form against detractors, and convince readers of playgoing's moral worth—but as Thomas Heywood (1570s–1641), himself a prolific writer of history plays, puts it:

---

[3] *Thomas of Woodstock, or Richard the Second, Part One*, ed. Peter Corbin and Douglas Sedge (Manchester: Manchester University Press, 2009).

[4] Benjamin Griffin, *Playing the Past: Approaches to English Historical Drama, 1386–1600* (Woodbridge: Boydell and Brewer, 2001), 76.

To turn to our domestic histories, what English blood, seeing the person of any bold English man presented and doth not hug his fame, and honey at his valor, pursuing him in his enterprise with his best wishes, and as being wrapt in contemplation, offers to him in his heart all prosperous performance [...] so bewitching a thing is lively and well spirited action, that it hath power to new mold the hearts of the spectators and fashion them to the shape of any noble and notable attempt.[5]

Heywood directs his reader's attention not to what the play might teach the audience about the events of the past, but how it might transform their hearts and minds in the present, how the characters of the drama can provide models to directly emulate here and now. Emotions, not facts, are the focus.

Some Elizabethan courtiers supposedly took this idea very literally. The most famous performance of *Richard II* offers a tantalizing glimpse of the possible connection between politics and performance in the Elizabethan period. When ambitious, but perhaps not strategically brilliant, aristocrat Robert Devereux, earl of Essex, attempted a coup against Queen Elizabeth I in 1601, one of his associates paid the Lord Chamberlain's Men, Shakespeare's acting company, to put on a special performance of *Richard II*. Sir Francis Bacon's account of the trial reports that

the afternoon before the Rebellion, [Sir Gilly] Merrick, with a great company of others, that afterwards were all in the action, had procured to be played before them, the play of deposing King Richard the second.

Neither was it casual, but a play bespoken by Merrick.

And not so only, but when it was told him by one of the Players, that the Play was old, and they should have loss in playing it, because few would come to it: there was forty shillings extraordinary given to play it, and so thereupon play'd it was.

So earnest he was to satisfy his eyes with the sight of that tragedy, which he thought soon after his Lord [Essex] should bring from the stage to the state, but that God turned it upon their own heads.[6]

---

[5] Thomas Heywood, *An Apology for actors* (London: Printed by Nicholas Okes, 1612), Early English Books Online Text Creation Partnership, http://name.umdl.umich.edu/A03185.0001.001. Spelling modernized.

[6] Francis Bacon, *A declaration of the practises & treasons attempted and committed by Robert late Earle of Essex and his complices* (London: printed by Robert Barker, 1601), Folger Shakespeare Library, STC 1133, doi.org/10.37078/230; Paul E. J. Hammer provides a recent re-evaluation of the incident in 'Shakespeare's *Richard II*, the Play of 7 February 1601, and the Essex Rising', *Shakespeare Quarterly* 15.9 (2008), 1–35. Spelling modernized.

Popular retellings of this story propose a secondary motive: 'to new mold the hearts of the spectators and fashion them to the shape of any noble and notable attempt', as Heywood would say and, hopefully, inspire the crowds to mimic the play's deposition of a weak and childless ruler. This gave rise to a possibly apocryphal story of Queen Elizabeth being told about the performance and responding, 'I am Richard II, know you not that?'[7] The association between Elizabeth and Richard makes for a tidy and exciting story, and a perfect reminder that we, like the Elizabethans, learn history through rumours and anecdotes often more thrilling than true.

Playwrights, too, were more concerned with telling a good story than faithfully replicating whatever hodgepodge of historical knowledge an audience might have. Facts could always be discarded in favour of drama, and that meant that any knowledge an audience member brought in with them could be rendered irrelevant by narrative expediency. Expecting to see King Richard's first wife, Anne of Bohemia? Or his six-year-old second queen Isabella? Both expectations would not only be thwarted by Shakespeare, but entirely irrelevant to the drama he was presenting. Shakespeare couldn't make assumptions about what an audience might be expecting or assuming—or at least, not in any way that his story relied upon. By necessity, *Richard II*—like all history plays—contains all the information an audience member would need to understand its basic narrative. Naturally, those with a rich knowledge of English history from whatever source might understand certain references in more depth, but the same could be said of those who were familiar with the narrative or poetic source materials of Shakespeare's comedies and tragedies, as well.

The idea that an audience member must understand the facts to understand the story not only assumes that said facts were shared collective knowledge, which we can see they were not—but also the idea that 'facts' themselves were of paramount importance. For Elizabethan readers and playgoers, 'historical accuracy' was not a concept that was as clear-cut or as important as it is for us. Even the chronicle

---

[7] After years of acceptance as fact, the connection between *Richard II* and Essex has been increasingly challenged. Jason Scott-Warren argues in favour of the veracity of this quotation in 'Was Elizabeth I Richard II?: The Veracity of Lambarde's "Conversation" ', *Review of English Studies* 64.264 (2013), 208–30, in the process of laying out the arguments against it.

histories such as those produced by Edward Hall and Raphael Holinshed, often referenced as fairly authoritative documents on par with history textbooks of today, were what seems to a modern reader to be a preposterous blend of fact, rumour, speculation, and outright myth. But it is more than a matter of more relaxed standards for sourcing: the expectation of accuracy itself simply was not the same, and this was naturally even more true of fictionalized material like ballads, poems, and plays.[8]

In fact, *Richard II* is one of the least clear examples of this out of all of Shakespeare's history plays, which may contribute to its reputation as too embedded in history to be readily understood. The history plays that come immediately after in Shakespeare's career, *Henry IV Part 1* and *Part 2*, provide a better demonstration. The most famous character of those plays is Sir John Falstaff, the heavy-drinking, morally flexible knight who keeps company with Prince Hal, the titular king's son, as he neglects his royal responsibilities. The then-popular legend of the future King Henry V as an irresponsible wastrel in his youth was likewise entirely untrue, but that did not stop the tale from forming the basis for at least two plays in the Elizabethan period, and from giving rise to one of Shakespeare's most iconic characters. King Henry IV and the future King Henry V were naturally both real people, and the plays depict some real events in their lives alongside the fictional ones, but Falstaff is, for all intents and purposes, entirely fictional. Elizabethan viewers saw no tension in this fictional character living alongside, and indeed ultimately dominating, a play nominally based on actual history.

Richard III is another example from earlier in Shakespeare's career. The most obvious fictionalized element is King Richard III himself, depicted in keeping with Tudor myth—the founding king of the Tudor dynasty having overthrown him in order to claim the English throne—as a hunchbacked psychopath. Richard's reign was not the chaotic spree of violence that Shakespeare's play suggests, and even the few scenes that are more or less true in their events are warped by their depiction through the powerful lens of Shakespeare's charismatic but wicked anti-hero. And then, of course, there are the ghosts. The play is threaded through with curses and prophecies, and culminates in Richard being

---

[8] Dermot Cavanagh, amongst others, argues this case in *Language and Politics in the Sixteenth-Century History Play* (Basingstoke: Palgrave Macmillan, 2003).

haunted by the ghosts of those he has killed, his confidence sapped on the eve of the play's decisive battle by their ill-wishes. Again, there is no tension here between history and fantasy. The presence of the ghosts did not make *Richard III* fundamentally different in Elizabethan eyes from the more emotionally grounded and realistic *Richard II*. This changed as the seventeenth century went on, but in the late 1590s, the lines were still wonderfully, bewilderingly blurred.

A Dynasty Crumbling

In the opening scene of *Richard II*, we are presented with something of a mystery: who is to blame for the murder of the Duke of Gloucester, King Richard's uncle? It is not immediately obvious that this is what the play's first scene is about. Richard's cousin, Harry Bolingbroke, has come to accuse another aristocrat, Thomas Mowbray, of treason. Bolingbroke lays out his accusations in a dramatically satisfying set of three, building from least to most important, and least to most attention-grabbing:

> Look what I speak, my life shall prove it true:
> That Mowbray hath received eight thousand nobles
> In name of lendings for your highness's soldiers,
> The which he hath detained for lewd employments,
> Like a false traitor and injurious villain.
> [...]
> Further I say, and further will maintain
> Upon his bad life to make all this good,
> That he did plot the Duke of Gloucester's death,
> Suggest his soon-believing adversaries,
> And consequently, like a traitor-coward,
> Sluiced out his innocent soul through streams of blood;
> Which blood, like sacrificing Abel's cries,
> Even from the tongueless caverns of the earth,
> To me for justice and rough chastisement:
> And, by the glorious worth of my descent,
> This arm shall do it, or this life be spent.
> (1.1.87–91, 98–108)

The final accusation carries the most emotional weight and is given almost twice as many lines. Mowbray, in contrast, brushes past it with

speed, sandwiching it between two lengthier passages of rebuttal—
but in the process, creates his speech's only rhymed couplet, drawing
special attention to this particular accusation once more: 'I slew him
not, but to my own disgrace | Neglected my sworn duty in that case'
(1.1.133–4).

Richard jumps in to try and defuse the conflict, cutting off any
further elaboration of this or any other alleged crimes. But Mowbray
and Bolingbroke hold firm, and Richard loses patience: 'We were not
born to sue, but to command' (1.1.196), he declares, and orders the
two men to meet for a trial by combat to resolve this. That Richard
has, in allowing this, utterly failed to command his two subjects goes
unremarked upon.

Though references to their shared past and convoluted crimes fly
between the Bolingbroke and Mowbray, Shakespeare is careful to
place the emotional and lyrical weight on the most important accusation: the murder. The tangled shared backstory of Bolingbroke and
Mowbray is irrelevant beyond this accusation, and in the next scene,
Shakespeare ensures that we know that. What begins as one item in
Bolingbroke's list of treasonous actions—an odd spare bullet point
that nobody seems to be taking very seriously, considering one lord is
accusing another of murdering the king's own uncle—blooms suddenly into a much deeper conspiracy as the play retreats from a public
accusation to a private one between its first and second scenes.

This, in fact, is the shape of the play's entire first act: a scene of
public ceremony is immediately complicated, and sometimes even
entirely undermined, by the scene of private conversation that follows.
From the play's first scene, where Bolingbroke's passionate reference
is buried in other speeches, one accusation among many, we transition
to a scene of just two characters: Gloucester's widow and Bolingbroke's
father, John of Gaunt. The Duchess of Gloucester brings the blaze of
narrowly focused righteous fury that the first scene lacks, demanding
that Gaunt help bring to justice the real force behind Gloucester's
murder: King Richard himself. Scholar Molly Smith writes:

The early scene involving the Duchess of Gloucester is deliberately placed
to interrupt the ceremonious scenes at court involving the conflict between
Mowbray and Bolingbroke. Its theatrical position heralds its status as an
alternate vision [...] [T]he Duchess sees the death of the Duke of Gloucester
as a familial violation demanding revenge from kin. Her pain, expressed
through metaphors and images which stress the familial bond, remains

unheeded by Gaunt, whose emphasis, like that of most of the males in the play, focuses on political ideology surrounding the divinity and sanctity of the monarch.[9]

Suddenly, after just one scene, the mystery isn't a mystery at all. It's a story about royal power, and how it can be abused.

Or can it? Gaunt protests that there is no possible way for a subject to bring justice against Richard, or against any king at all: 'God's is the quarrel, for God's substitute, | His deputy anointed in his sight, | Hath caused [Gloucester's] death, the which if wrongfully, | Let heaven revenge, for I may never lift | An angry arm against his minister' (1.2.37–41). Chosen by God, Richard's choices are God's choices. While Gaunt leaves open the possibility that heaven could avenge Gloucester, the fundamental logical conclusion of his argument is that a king can do no wrong. One way of reading *Richard II* as a whole is as a thought experiment in response to this idea, a dynastic tragedy that pulls taut and tests the breaking point of the tension between divine and human agency. Who is really in charge here: people, or God?[10] Anthony B. Dawson and Paul Yachnin ask in their 2011 introduction to the text for The Oxford Shakespeare, 'How powerful can the play's oppositional argument be when it seems to bend so much of its dramatic energy and formal properties of action, characterization, and imagery towards making us weep for the death of the King?'.[11] And yet, said King himself never ceases to insist on his own potential divinity.

With the Duchess of Gloucester's revelation, Richard's desire to reconcile Bolingbroke and Mowbray rather than allowing their accusations to be publicly judged takes on a new meaning, as does his abject failure to get his angry subjects under control. We return to a scene of great pomp and ceremony, the promised duel between

---

[9] Molly Smith, 'Minor Scenes and "Mutant" Conflicts in *Richard II*', in Dympna Callaghan (ed.), *A Feminist Companion to Shakespeare* (Malden: Blackwell, 2016), 281–93 (284).

[10] These competing interpretations of the play itself have also been influentially articulated by Ernst Kantorowicz, *The King's Two Bodies* (Princeton: Princeton University Press, 1957) and Rebecca Lemon, *Treason by Words: Literature, Law, and Rebellion in Shakespeare's England* (New York: Cornell University Press, 2011). Ivo Kamps suggests in *Historiography and Ideology in Stuart Drama* (Cambridge: Cambridge University Press, 1997), 125–55, that Richard is a deliberate example of a monarch's failure to navigate these contradictory imperatives.

[11] *Richard II*, ed. Paul Yachnin and Anthony B. Dawson (Oxford: Oxford University Press, 2011), 28.

Bolingbroke and Mowbray. This is a fight that is designed not to demonstrate their fighting prowess, but to see whose side of the dispute has the support of God. Tension mounts as the combatants perform ritualized entrances, greetings, farewells to their loved ones. 'God' is invoked thirteen times in the first half of the scene in formal, repetitive recitations: Mowbray calls upon 'the grace of God, and this mine arm, | To prove [Bolingbroke], in defending of myself, | A traitor to my God, my king, and me, | And as I truly fight, defend me heaven!' (1.3.22–5); and Bolingbroke answers, 'who ready here do stand in arms | To prove by God's grace, and my body's valour | In lists on Thomas Mowbray, Duke of Norfolk, | That he is a traitor foul and dangerous | To God of heaven, King Richard, and to me; | And as I truly fight, defend me heaven!' (1.3.36–41). In short: Jesus, take the lance!

And then, after all this mirrored ritual, the preparations of the combatants, the places taken, and the lances raised—King Richard stops it all in its tracks. A quick conference with his courtiers, and the duel is cancelled just as it begins. The new sentence: exile for both parties. A ceremony designed to demonstrate the will of God disrupted by God's deputy, the answer to the question of Gloucester's murder deliberately delayed and obscured by the man accused of committing it. Who is really in charge here: Richard, or God?

Thus, we open the play with the image of a kingdom undermined, two scenes of public display of royal power that foreshadow the events to come. Richard twice utterly fails to manage his unruly nobles, and resorts to sweeping gestures of divinely sanctioned autocracy to keep things in line. Shakespeare is quick to crack the smooth façade, showing us first the grieving and angry Duchess of Gloucester and, through her, the truth of what Richard is attempting to hide. Then, the moving and mournful farewell between the exiled Bolingbroke and his elderly father Gaunt is instantly undercut by a glimpse of Richard himself in private with his favourites, a gaggle of gossips. Another royal relative, Aumerle, Richard and Bolingbroke's other first cousin, sneers at the departed Bolingbroke. He and Richard mock their cousin's departure and scheme how to steal his inheritance to fund Richard's planned wars in Ireland.[12] Richard simultaneously is

---

[12] Martha A. Kurtz traces the use of such sardonic humour throughout the play in '"Mock not": The Problem of Laughter in *Richard II*', *University of Toronto Quarterly* 65.4 (1996), 584–99.

abusing his power and cannot keep his kingdom under control. The truth keeps sneaking out from behind the ceremony. He is God's deputy and his every choice is thus divinely sanctioned; yet, for some reason, other people keep on pursuing their own agendas, much to the king's annoyance. But the exile of Bolingbroke has, in addition to ridding the court of an irritant, opened up useful possibilities. God still seems to smile on Richard: John of Gaunt is dying, and that provides the perfect opportunity to snatch up his estates for the enrichment of the crown.

There has been a change in Gaunt, a man who in many ways symbolizes England itself. A scene ago, he told a grieving widow, his sister-in-law, that there could be no redress for her loss. 'Where then, alas, may I complain myself?' she asked, and he replied, 'To God, the widow's champion and defence' (1.2.42–3). At the end of the abortive duel, in grief himself at the imminent loss of his son, his worldview subtly seems to shift, and he observes the extent of royal power with a new awareness both of its arbitrary reach and of its limits.[13] Richard, in supposed deference to Gaunt's sorrow, suddenly reduces the term of Bolingbroke's banishment by four years. Bolingbroke marvels, perhaps somewhat sarcastically, 'Four lagging winters and four wanton springs | End in a word, such is the breath of kings' (1.3.212–13). But where Bolingbroke is fixated on the power of kingship, his father suddenly sees its shortcomings: 'Shorten my days thou canst with sullen sorrow, | And pluck nights from me, but not lend a morrow. | Thou canst help time to furrow me with age, | But stop no wrinkle in his pilgrimage. | Thy word is current with him for my death, | But dead, thy kingdom cannot buy my breath' (1.3.225–30). The spell is broken: Gaunt is no longer cowed by what Richard is permitted to do, but strangely, if morosely, liberated by thoughts of what even a king cannot achieve.

Gaunt carries this new cynicism into the second act and his final scene, where he delivers one of Shakespeare's most famous and most misapplied speeches, one that establishes him as a voice for the shifting views of the country itself. Far from accepting the role of passive

---

[13] John Michael Archer proposes in 'Fruits of Duty: Honor in Shakespeare's *King Richard II*', *Modern Language Notes* 135.5 (2020), 1170–83, that Richard's failure to console Gaunt and to control Mowbray and Bolingbroke in the play's first scene are essential reflections of a growing cultural awareness of such royal limitations. A king cannot give life; nor can he even give honour.

observer of God's will enacted through Richard, Gaunt now sees himself, not Richard, as the holy vessel of truth: 'Methinks I am a prophet new inspired' (2.1.31), he declares as he delivers a eulogy for England as he knew it—'This royal throne of kings, this sceptred isle, | This earth of majesty, this seat of Mars, | This other Eden, demi-paradise' (2.1.40–2). Now, far from seeing him as God's untouchable substitute, Gaunt takes Richard to task for his profligacy and his treatment of the country: 'Landlord of England art thou now, not king' (2.1.113).

Gaunt refers here specifically to Richard's financial mismanagement of the country and the bargains he's cut to give land and power to his favourites, but the language Shakespeare gives him also reflects a reimagined relationship between ruler and country. There is no divine, unbreakable bond between a landlord and the land; he is simply the person put in charge of it. A landlord's actions carry no holy sanction. He can misuse and abuse his land; and if he does, he can be criticized for his treatment of it. He can sell it—or have it taken from him. It is the first direct iteration of a metaphor that threads throughout the play and will recur with more force in the next act: is the king God, or a gardener? That is to say, is he inextricably bonded to his title and his land, or is he merely a caretaker of both?[14]

This is also only the first blow struck against the solidity of Richard's identity as king in this scene. Gaunt challenges Richard's bond to his kingdom, and when Gaunt dies, Richard's last surviving uncle, York, tentatively prods at Richard's right to claim it at all. He doesn't mean to—far from it—but it is Richard himself who forces the comparison by seizing all of Gaunt's land and titles, effectively disinheriting the exiled Bolingbroke. York is appalled on moral grounds, but cannot help but point out the problematic precedent Richard is setting: if he does this, 'Be not thyself, for how art thou a king | But by fair sequence and succession?' (2.1.199–200). York, who has stood silently by throughout the first two acts—who freely admits that 'Not Gloucester's death, nor [Bolingbroke]'s banishment, | Nor Gaunt's rebukes, nor England's private wrongs, | [...] nor my own disgrace, | Have ever made me sour my patient cheek, | Or bend one wrinkle on my sovereign's face' (2.1.166–71)—is stopped short

---

[14] See Marjorie Garber, 'Richard II', in *Shakespeare After All* (New York: Random House, 2004), 238–69.

by an action that would undermine Richard's very right to act. If the line of succession between father and son can be broken on a whim, then there is nothing underpinning Richard's claim to the throne. There is no way to be sure that he really was chosen by God, born into his position by holy will. A landlord, not God's substitute.

With Gaunt dead, York takes up his mantle as both Richard's would-be counsellor and, despite himself, increasingly disillusioned reflection of Richard's weakening grip on power. This is crystallized when Richard departs Gaunt's deathbed for war in Ireland, one of centuries' worth of English attempts solidify their grip on Ireland and crush native resistance to their rule—an effort that would feel very timely to Shakespeare's audiences, then embroiled in their own iteration of the conflict.

Richard names York as regent while he is away. As soon as Richard leaves, Bolingbroke—who, we learn, has been lying in wait for this opportunity—returns, now with his disinheritance as an excuse for breaking his vow to remain in exile as ordered. York comes to intercept him when he lands, demanding an explanation and asserting his power as Richard's substitute: 'Com'st thou because the anointed King is hence? | Why, foolish boy, the King is left behind, | And in my loyal bosom lies his power' (2.3.95–7). But in his very next lines, York admits that the body that contains this kingly power isn't as young or strong as it used to be, and by the end of the scene, fully capitulates: 'my power is weak and all ill left' (2.3.153). His show of royal strength was no more than a bluff. If the king's power is contained within York, then that power is feeble and impotent, a foreshadowing of failures to come.

Act 3 zeroes in on the image of God and the gardener to try and understand the nature of Richard's power. Richard returns to England and physically embraces the shoreline, calling upon the land itself to 'Throw death upon thy sovereign's enemies [...] This earth shall have a feeling, and these stones | Prove armèd soldiers ere her native king | Shall falter under foul rebellion's arms' (3.2.22, 24–6). The Bishop of Carlisle, who accompanies him, agrees, 'That power that made you king | Hath power to keep you king in spite of all' (3.2.27–8). But this opening display of faith is immediately shaken by news of Bolingbroke's strength, the defection of Richard's armies, the mood of the people. Like the tides they stand before, Richard's confidence ebbs and flows, first declaring that 'Not all the water in the rough rude sea | Can wash the balm off from a 'nointed king' (3.2.54–5), a reference to the holy oil that is applied to a monarch during his coronation. But shortly thereafter, he sinks to the ground in despair to 'tell sad stories of the death of kings' (3.2.156). Every source of hope is swiftly dashed, every rise in spirits followed by a dramatic fall. The speed with which these changes take place is almost comic, as is the relentlessness of the barrage of bad news; but in constraining these dramatic turns to a single turbulent scene, Shakespeare emphasizes Richard's powerlessness, his complete lack of agency or direction. He has Richard insist that 'when this thief, this traitor, Bolingbroke, | Who all this while hath revelled in the night [. . .] | Shall see us rising in our throne, the east, | His treasons will sit blushing in his face, | Not able to endure the sight of day, | But, self-affrighted, tremble at his sin' (3.2.47–8, 50–3). Richard's power, as awesome and natural as the sun, will drive away Bolingbroke on sight. But Bolingbroke, in contrast, has been hard at work, and the endless stream of bad news is the fruit not of the unsolicited intervention of the land of England itself, but Bolingbroke's own activity and labour. Richard waits for God; Bolingbroke has 'sworn to weed and pluck away' (2.3.166) the excesses of Richard's reign, and in response, 'Both young and old rebel' (3.2.119) to his cause. One turns to God, the other makes himself a gardener.

If only, laments an old palace gardener, Richard had 'so trimmed and dressed his land | As we this garden!' (3.4.57–8). Spinning out an extended and rather blunt simile, the gardener and his assistant reveal Richard's capture and forthcoming deposition, proposing that it is a direct result not of Bolingbroke's strength, but of Richard's own failure to manage the country properly. Far from the earth rising to assist him, the land's neglect is the cause of Richard's downfall. The ghost of Gaunt appears here in some contemporary productions, as directors double-cast the actor playing Gaunt as the gardener, as in Michael Boyd's production for the Royal Shakespeare Company in 2007. Now a very different kind of caretaker, with this casting, Gaunt speaks the fulfilment of his own prophecy. In the image of the king as gardener, Shakespeare suggests another essential dimension to the question of the limits of Richard's power: not only must we ask whether Richard is allowed to act with total impunity because he is chosen by God; but if he is not, what specifically is a king's duty of care to his country and his people? What is all that power *for*? These were questions that could not safely be asked of the actual monarch in Shakespeare's day, but could find expression onstage in stories of the past.

Act 3 is equally notable for what Shakespeare does not, or cannot, show. This 'cannot' is partly literal: one of the crucial elements of *Richard II*'s textual history is the excision for print of the scene where Richard publicly hands over his crown to Bolingbroke.[15] But as the scene with the gardeners demonstrates, there is a strange skipped step within the narrative as well.

Bolingbroke arrives in England insisting that his only goal is to reclaim his stolen inheritance, a fact he reiterates again and again. And yet, somewhere between his landing in Act 2, scene 3; Richard's self-surrender into his custody at the end of Act 3, scene 3; and the gardeners' conversation in Act 3, scene 4, the discussion changes. 'What, think you the King shall be deposed?' the gardener's assistant asks, and the gardener replies, 'Depressed he is already, and deposed | 'Tis doubt he will be' (3.4.68–70). When York enters partway through the next scene, the deal is all but done:

YORK   Great Duke of Lancaster, I come to thee
  From plume-plucked Richard, who with willing soul
  Adopts thee heir, and his high sceptre yields
  To the possession of thy royal hand.
  Ascend his throne, descending now from him,
  And long live Henry, fourth of that name!

BOLINGBROKE   In God's name I'll ascend the regal throne.

(4.1.107–13)

Though one protest is lodged, it is clear from the rest of the scene to follow that this is not an unexpected announcement, and Richard is summoned to ceremonially enact what he has already promised. Much is made of the fact that this was, supposedly, Richard's choice: 'do that office of thine own good will | Which tired majesty did make thee offer' (4.1.175–8), York urges, and Bolingbroke, ever laconic, replies

---

[15] This fact has been analysed extensively, including debates about whether the scene was cut for print, or added later; see the New Oxford Shakespeare Critical Reference Edition (357ff). See also David Bergeron, 'The Deposition Scene in *Richard II*', *Renaissance Papers 1974* (1975), 31–7, and Cyndia Susan Clegg, ' "By the choise and intimation of all the realme": *Richard II* and Elizabethan Press Censorship', *Shakespeare Quarterly* 48.1 (1997), 432–48, for two perspectives.

to Richard's first mournful monologue by stating, 'I thought you had been willing to resign' (4.1.189). Richard has already pointed out that Bolingbroke's armies have somewhat curtailed his options ('They well deserve to have | That know the strong'st and surest way to get' [3.3.198–9])—and yet, deposition was supposedly never Bolingbroke's goal. When and how did this change? Why did Richard choose to offer it, and why did Bolingbroke accept? An actor or audience member can read between the lines and conjure up any number of stories to fill in the gaps, but on the page, the gap remains. It is as if, when faced with having to actually answer the questions the play has posed up to this point—whether it is God's design or men's actions that shape history; the rights of a king versus the limits of his power; God and the gardener—Shakespeare suddenly balked. For all of these questions coalesce in the act that Richard and Bolingbroke undertake in this scene, and their potential answers define that act's legitimacy. Can Richard actually be deposed? Is it possible for a man to stop being king, and for another one to take his place, or is he irrevocably anointed by God no matter how he behaves or how badly he lets down his kingdom—even, indeed, if his kingdom doesn't want him anymore?

At the very centre of the play, in the moments that seem to be building up to finally to answer its central question, Shakespeare instead looks away. How can a king be deposed, if indeed he can be at all? What goes into that choice, what makes it possible, what does that seismic and impossible moment look like and sound like, embodied by performers enacting that shift before your eyes? *Richard II* will not, cannot, show you.

Fathers and Sons

When Bolingbroke challenges Mowbray at the beginning of the play, never far from anyone's thoughts is the fact that Bolingbroke is Richard's first cousin. Not next in line to the throne but also not far from it. Mowbray, Richard, and Bolingbroke himself, repeatedly invoke the royalty of Bolingbroke's blood, most often in the form of disclaiming it: 'Setting aside his high blood's royalty, | And let him be no kinsman to my liege, | I do defy him' (1.1.58–60), says Mowbray in his opening accusation. But, of course, all these protestations serve to do is to remind the listener of the impossibility of ever really erasing Bolingbroke's nobility and proximity to the crown. It is also a reminder, repeated again and again in the opening moments of the play, that this is a story about a family.

In the play's second scene, the Duchess of Gloucester conjures the image of a branching family tree, with the sons of the previous king, Edward III, its many offshoots. Her murdered husband, she says, is a broken branch, 'hacked down, and his summer leaves all faded' (1.2.20). There are three surviving branches highlighted in the play: John of Gaunt, who holds the title of the Duke of Lancaster, and his son Bolingbroke; the Duke of York and his son Aumerle; and, of course, Richard himself. As the play goes on, the two Dukes increasingly cannot resist making reference to the missing figure in this tidy trio of remaining branches of Edward III's tree: Richard's deceased father, Edward the Black Prince.[16]

The beginning and end of the play are both defined by fathers' relationships to their sons, and within this frame, Richard's lack of such a relationship feels increasingly stark. His father is not a person from whom he can seek emotional support, as Bolingbroke does, or even with whom he can feud, as Aumerle does. He exists for Richard only as an accusation, a legacy he is failing to uphold. It is, again, no accident that in only the second scene of the play, Shakespeare turns away from the public pageantry of Richard's court to reiterate that what we have just seen and what we are about to see is a familial conflict. The Duchess of Gloucester begs her brother-in-law Gaunt to remember his fraternal ties, to defy his king in service of his brother. In that scene, Gaunt refuses. But Richard's attack on his own small family, the exile of Gaunt's son, dislodges Gaunt's faith in the infallibility of the monarch, and as he is dying, his mind returns to his deceased father and brothers:

> O, spare me not, my brother Edward's son,
> For that I was his father Edward's son.
> That blood already, like the pelican,
> Hast thou tapped out and drunkenly caroused.
> My brother Gloucester, plain well-meaning soul,
> Whom fair befall in heaven 'mongst happy souls,
> May be a precedent and witness good
> That thou respect'st not spilling Edward's blood.
>
> (2.1.125–32)

---

[16] Fred B. Tromly provides an analysis of this 'generation gap' in *Fathers and Sons in Shakespeare: The Debt Never Promised* (Toronto: University of Toronto Press, 2010).

Gaunt envisions Richard as a pelican, a bird proverbially believed to kill its parent by drinking her blood, echoing the Duchess of Gloucester's image of 'Edward's seven sons [. . .] as seven vials of his sacred blood', now 'cracked, and all the precious liquor spilt' (1.2.11–12, 19). But Gaunt's simile goes a step farther, envisioning that shared blood not as spilled and wasted, but consumed by Richard. Not just a disappointment in his treatment of his country, Gaunt also accuses Richard of destroying his own family. This, indeed, is the last accusation he makes before laying a curse on Richard and departing the stage to die.

Such a blend of political and familial responsibility is taken up by York at the end of the scene. In his shock at Richard's decision to seize Gaunt's land and goods, his first thoughts are not of the social implications, but rather—echoing Gaunt—of his family: 'I am the last of noble Edward's sons, | Of whom thy father, Prince of Wales, was first' (2.1.172–3), he begins, and goes on to describe the deceased Prince of Wales in detail for the first time in the play, praising his prowess in battle and his loyalty to his allies. He concludes, 'O Richard, York is too far gone with grief, | Or else he never would compare between' (2.1.185–6), and Richard does not seem to notice, or chooses to ignore, his words—but, for the reader and viewer, the protestation comes too late. Shakespeare embeds once more an instant reminder that for all the broader political import of Richard's actions, all the questions raised about the limits of his divine right as king, the very first thing to remember is that he is doing this in front of his uncle, a man who has just watched his last surviving brother die while cursing his nephew's name.

York is again the vessel for such fleeting, but deliberate, reminders of the characters' deep connections when he learns of the death of his sister-in-law, the Duchess of Gloucester. He bustles onto the scene already left reeling by the news of Bolingbroke's arrival in England and Richard's departure for Ireland, all while '[h]ere am I left to underprop his land, | Who, weak with age, cannot support myself' (2.2.82–3). As he rattles off problems to solve, a messenger enters with news that seems to have no context: 'My lord, your son was gone before I came' (2.2.86). York quickly moves past the moment, and we will not entirely learn what it means until later in the act: that York's son Aumerle has immediately departed for Richard's side, a decision that will set father and son, somewhat unwillingly on York's part, on opposite sides of the conflict between Richard and Bolingbroke.

The same messenger brings worse news, however: the Duchess of Gloucester is dead. York seems overwhelmed by this final blow: 'I know not what to do. I would to God, | So my untruth had not provoked him to it, | The King had cut off my head with my brother's' (2.2.100–2). The blunt but plaintive half-line—'I know not what to do'—stands out starkly in a scene that has so far been defined by convoluted speeches and imagery. York tries to return to business, but immediately gets muddled as he turns to Richard's queen: 'Come, sister—cousin I would say—pray pardon me' (2.2.105).

York manages to collect himself and usher everyone offstage with orders. But this momentary collapse into something bewildered and bereaved, mixing up the familial titles of the queen and the Duchess of Gloucester, is a flash of humanity—a small but deliberate detail that reminds us of Shakespeare's constant attentiveness in this play to the personal weight of its story for the characters. It comes at the end of a scene that encapsulates the other means by which Shakespeare embeds a family tragedy within a dynastic drama—or perhaps it is the other way around. For again and again, Shakespeare takes pains to reveal seismic change or dramatic turns of fortune through the lens of family ties, never permitting the drama to lose sight of the human cost of a conflict between cousins.

Female characters are often overlooked in history plays, but their presence always signals a deliberate change in perspective and often tone. The women of *Richard II* are no exception.[17] When Richard's queen—who is never named—enters at the beginning of Act 2, scene 2, she is weighed down by a sense of foreboding that she cannot quite define and that Richard's favourites, her companions, cannot understand. By the end of the scene, various other characters have arrived to act as—as the Queen puts it—'the midwife to [her] woe' (2.2.62), giving her nameless, shapeless fear a concrete form in the armed arrival of Bolingbroke to England and the defection of key allies to his cause. We learn that the earl of Northumberland and his son have joined Bolingbroke, and that Northumberland's brother, the steward

---

[17] I discuss this pattern generally, including in relation to Richard's queen, in *Staging Female Characters in Shakespeare's English History Plays* (Cambridge: Cambridge University Press, 2023); Molly Smith provides a particularly compelling reading of *Richard II* specifically in 'Minor Scenes and "Mutant" Conflicts in *Richard II*'.

of the king's household, has also fled to join them. But we aren't shown the scene of this traitorous departure of a key figure in the royal court—we are only given it to experience from the Queen's point of view, centring on her reactions to these events over their political or broader social repercussions. Literary critic Colleen Ruth Rosenfeld writes,

Instead of staging Bolingbroke's return [...] the Queen's conceit stages knowledge of this return. While it might seem that the absence of the event contributes to the historical perspective from which Bolingbroke has always already returned, the staging of this form of knowledge instead transforms the theater into the field of possibility within which Shakespeare's history transpires.[18]

In other words, the Queen's perspective on the world is one that contains not only the inevitable path of history laid out before the characters, but the possibilities of other outcomes that can only be expressed in the kind of poetic language her conversational partners so struggle to understand. It is a glimpse of a completely different way of thinking about history, but one Shakespeare only can sustain for a brief scene.

This is not the first time Shakespeare redirects our gaze in this manner, often using the play's female characters to do so. The early scene between the Duchess of Gloucester and John of Gaunt is one example; later, York's momentary pause to receive news about his son is echoed by the son himself when Richard returns from Ireland: 'Where is the Duke my father with his power?' (3.2.143), Aumerle demands, Shakespeare not neglecting an opportunity to remind us of the personal connections between the characters. He repeats himself shortly thereafter: 'My father hath a power. Enquire of him' (3.2.186), and this time is answered with the news that his father York has surrendered to Bolingbroke, the final stroke in the barrage of bad news that structures the scene.

The play's most earth-shaking decision is again not shown, but given to the Queen to hear. As she loiters in a garden, depressed and lost, she overhears the gossiping gardeners reveal that Richard is to be deposed. The Queen alludes to how radical this is as a narrative choice: 'Doth not thy embassage belong to me, | And am I last that

[18] Colleen Ruth Rosenfeld, 'The Queen's Conceit in *Richard II*', *Studies in English Literature* 60.1 (2020), 25–46 (30–1).

knows it?' (3.4.94–5). In a way, she speaks for and as the audience—
shouldn't *we* have been the first to know this, to see it happening?[19]
But we are instead pushed, with the Queen, away from the public
courts where Richard's allies turn on him, and into the intimacy and
quiet of the garden, where the Queen can claim this news not as the
political tides that shake the whole country, but as only her own tragedy. The news is revealed from the perspective of a woman who sees
it not as the downfall of a king, but the suffering of her husband.

This scene is echoed in the aftermath of Richard's fall, when we
learn about how 'rude misgoverned hands from windows' tops | Threw
dust and rubbish on King Richard's head' (5.2.5–6) when he and
Bolingbroke entered London after Richard's deposition. Or more
specifically, 'our two cousins' coming into London' (5.2.3)—for
Shakespeare once again does not miss a chance to frame a scene with
reminders of its players' consanguinity. We are not given the tragic
procession to watch, but instead hear the Duke of York describe it to
his wife. And, as the Duchess of York reminds the audience in the
scene's opening lines, she receives this news not as a disinterested
spectator, but as a direct relation of those involved. This gives way to
one of the play's strangest sequences, one that leads to Bolingbroke
himself to point out that 'our scene is altered from a serious thing'
(5.3.78) as the Duke and Duchess of York compete with each other in
comic fashion to respectively accuse and plead for their son Aumerle,
who is caught plotting against the newly crowned King Henry IV out
of lingering loyalty to Richard.[20]

The Duke argues—as John of Gaunt did all the way back in Act 1—
for complete objectivity. His son is a traitor, and so must be
punished. His wife is appalled—like the Duchess of Gloucester—that
York can be so devoid of family feeling. This repetition in an exagger-
ated register of the opening sequence's accusations of treason inter-
mingled with complicated family loyalties reflects the differences
between Richard and Bolingbroke's reigns: there is no elaborate
pageantry here, no backroom murders (yet). But Bolingbroke, too,
struggles to maintain control over the scene and its expression:

[19] Scott McMillin unpacks the use of the word 'unseen' in both Richard and his
Queen's journeys towards tragedy in 'Shakespeare's *Richard II:* Eyes of Sorrow, Eyes of
Desire', *Shakespeare Quarterly* 35 (1985), 40–52.
[20] Sheldon P. Zitner, 'Aumerle's Conspiracy', *Studies in English Literature* 14 (1974),
239–57, discusses the generic shifts that Aumerle engenders.

where Richard could not permit the carefully staged tournament to go forward for fear of its outcome, Bolingbroke's attempts to handle matters quietly descend into farce. Many twenty-first century productions make a misguided attempt to turn this scene back towards tragedy by having Aumerle come to murder Richard in the play's final scene, the implication being this is the unspoken price for his future safety. But this attempt to make the scene 'fit' into the tonal expectations of a historical drama undermines the scene and character's meaning. Even a king is reduced to helplessness in the face of the fractious demands of blood: the divided loyalty, the deep love. Bolingbroke can only sit on this throne not because he betrayed his king, but because he betrayed his cousin. The details of Aumerle's plot do not particularly matter as his parents fail to condemn or to save him—the point has always been that this is the tragedy of a kingdom, yes, but first it is the tragedy of a family.

As King Henry IV, Bolingbroke has problems that Richard never faced. Where Richard is dogged by the ghost of his father's legacy, the king that the Black Prince never got to be, Bolingbroke's new dawn is shadowed by fears about the king to come: his oldest son, Harry. Before the York parents barge in to plead for their son, Bolingbroke frets about his own: 'Can no man tell of my unthrifty son? | 'Tis full three months since I did see him last. | If any plague hang over us, 'tis he' (5.3.1–3). It is a tantalizing glimpse of the play yet to be written about this son, but it is also another entry in the pattern we have seen again and again. Glimpses, flashes, moments, reminders that the scaffolding of this story is family ties. But this does not mean that understanding the play rests inevitably upon intimate knowledge of some sprawling family tree. Imagine, instead, that it is an invitation to reject that mode of mapping relationships entirely, and focus on kinship, on feeling. While readers today can, in theory, look backwards from Shakespeare's *Henry IV* plays and immediately picture the character to whom Bolingbroke refers, those plays had not been written when those lines were first spoken. Shakespeare did not and could not assume they meant anything to a viewer except what they say: a father fretting about what his son will make of his legacy. What does it mean, dynastically, when the Duchess of York refers to Richard as 'cousin'? That matters less than that she sees herself as linked to him, that he has a place in her heart beyond that owed to a king by his courtier.

A story that begins with an accusation of murder of uncle by nephew ends with the murder of cousin by cousin. Overheard and misinterpreted, Bolingbroke finds himself responsible for the actions of an overzealous courtier, who has Richard killed because he believes it is what his new king secretly wants. And it *is*, but it was a wish the politically savvy Bolingbroke knew perfectly well never could, and never should, be fulfilled: 'Though I did wish him dead, | I hate the murderer, love him murderèd' (5.6.39–40). The syntax of the second line carries a double meaning: either that he loves the fact that Richard is murdered, or loves the man who was murdered, i.e. Richard, or—very likely—deliberately a little of both.

Henry banishes the murderer as he himself was once banished, and turns in anguish to the court: 'Lords, I protest my soul is full of woe | That blood should sprinkle me to make me grow' (5.6.45–6). But Bolingbroke is mistaken in thinking he could ever have risen any other way. This has always been a story about blood.

Richard *as Queer Tragedy*

Richard is a man who does not fit. He has not even fit here, so far. We have glanced at him through others' eyes. But Richard expands to fill the space he is given: grant him the spotlight and he will take it, to the exclusion of almost everything and everyone else. Richard's shock interruption of the trial by combat in the play's third scene sets up a pattern of behaviour that only grows more pronounced and dramatic as the story goes on. Richard seems unable to allow a scene to progress in the way it seems it ought to by custom or even by external narrative expectations—and his alterations to the script always seem to end with him at the centre of attention.

From early on, Richard is characterized by others in terms of excess, criticized for the way he transgresses expectations and boundaries. He spends too much money. His ear is too open to flattery, his hand too quick to reward his flatterers. The core of Gaunt's famous speech of complaint against Richard is not just nostalgia about a lost England, but criticism of the king's extravagance and financial mismanagement: 'A thousand flatterers sit within thy crown, | Whose compass is no bigger than thy head, | And yet encagèd in so small a verge | The waste is no whit lesser than thy land' (2.1.100–3). He calls Richard 'landlord' and makes repeated passing reference to the idea that England is 'leased out [...] Like to a tenement or pelting farm' (2.1.59–60). But the details of what Richard has done matter far less than the spirit of them, which is that Richard is wasteful and unseemly. Everything he does is *too much*—and yet also too little, when it comes to taking responsibility for the management of his country.

York concurs with Gaunt in both substance and style, complaining in the same scene, 'Where doth the world thrust forth a vanity— | So it be new, there's no respect how vile— | That is not quickly buzzed into his ears?' (2.1.24–6). Richard's capacious appetite for novelty, for wonders from all over the world, stands in stark contrast to his uncle's reverence for the 'little world' (2.1.45) of England. Richard does not want to be, or cannot be, contained within 'This precious stone set in the silver sea, | Which serves it in the office of a wall, | Or as a moat defensive to a house' (2.1.46–8). The image Gaunt conjures is beautiful, but it is also parochial and deliberately insular. Richard's eyes wander elsewhere—certainly to Ireland, where he has colonial ambitions. But he seems to strain the bounds of Gaunt's little island in less literal ways, too—a subtle prelude to a tragedy that will see the perimeter of his world shrink smaller and smaller, until a mere coffin can contain it.[21]

This excess and yearning, this 'rash, fierce blaze of riot' (2.1.33), is something we hear about, but never quite see.[22] Though we do watch Richard's impetuousness—in stopping the trial by combat—and his greed—seizing Gaunt's money and land—when he is faced with a genuine crisis upon his return to England, he slips into a curious passivity that openly frustrates his followers. Like his uncles, they expect something other than what Richard is willing or able to give: an image of leadership he is only intermittently able to achieve. Much later in the play, just before he is imprisoned, Richard's Queen berates him for his capitulation:

[21] Margaret Tudeau-Clayton discusses in *Shakespeare's Englishes: Against Englishness* (Cambridge: Cambridge University Press, 2019) how discourses of the period contrasted idealized Englishness—and especially idealized masculinity—against such fascination with foreign fads.

[22] Judith Brown connects this loss of unseen pleasure to Richard's fundamental queerness, discussed more below, in 'Pretty Richard (In Three Parts)', in Madhavi Menon, ed., *Shakesqueer* (Durham, NC: Duke University Press, 2011), 286–93.

What, is my Richard both in shape and mind
Transformed and weakened? Hath Bolingbroke
Deposed thine intellect? Hath he been in thy heart?
The lion dying thrusteth forth his paw
And wounds the earth, if nothing else, with rage
To be o'er-powered; and wilt thou, pupil-like,
Take the correction, mildly kiss the rod,
And fawn on rage with base humility,
Which art a lion and the king of beasts?

(5.1.26–34)

But this pattern of behaviour first appeared long before, when Richard sat on the English shore receiving blow after blow to his hopes of defeating Bolingbroke. His cousin Aumerle pleads that 'we are too remiss, | Whilst Bolingbroke, through our security, | Grows strong and great in power and account' (3.2.33–5). But Richard is secure indeed, reminding Aumerle that 'For every man that Bolingbroke hath pressed | To lift shrewd steel against our golden crown, | God for his Richard hath in heavenly pay | A glorious angel' (3.2.58–61). And even when it becomes clear that God's angels have not appeared to slow Bolingbroke's triumph, Richard's response is not 'rage | To be o'er-powered' as the Queen urges later, but something much more like despair.[23]

Richard's answer to adversity is not to look forward to what can yet be done, but backwards, to the past. He wants to 'talk of graves, of worms, and epitaphs', to 'sit upon the ground | And tell sad stories of the death of kings' (3.2.145, 155–6).[24] When his every attempt to rally in this scene is swiftly beaten back by more bad news of Bolingbroke's success, Richard gives up—though, notably, his allies do not. Aumerle tries to the end to get through to Richard, and as we've just seen, even when all is lost, the Queen still urges some form of defiance, even if it is hollow. 'Yet looks he like a king' (3.3.67), York

---

[23] Zenón Luis-Martínez's 'Shakespeare's Historical Drama as *Traurspiel: Richard II—And After*', *English Literary History* 75.3 (2008), 673–705, compellingly proposes reading Richard's story as a 'mourning play' in the style proposed by Walter Benjamin, arguing that 'the mournful experience of history is essential' to this play and its sequels (674).

[24] See Jonathan Baldo's *Memory in Shakespeare's Histories: Stages of Forgetting* (London: Routledge, 2011) for an analysis of how 'Richard is transformed from a monarch who is defined largely by his studied neglect of the past to an embodiment of painful historical awareness' (11).

sighs when Richard enters on the walls of a castle to greet Bolingbroke's ally Northumberland and, briefly, chastise him. But what York laments as 'so fair a show' (3.3.70) proves to be *merely* a show indeed: despite looking like a king, and briefly sounding like one, Richard immediately gives in; his thunderous accusations that 'God omnipotent, | Is mustering in his clouds on our behalf | Armies of pestilence; and they shall strike | Your children yet unborn and unbegot' (3.3.84–7) give way with startling speed to the promise that Bolingbroke 'is right welcome hither, | And all the number of his fair demands | Shall be accomplished without contradiction' (3.3.121–3). By the end of the scene, he has promised to enter London in Bolingbroke's custody.

His Queen, his uncles, his allies—no one can easily see past what Richard ought to be and to who he really is. And Richard himself, for all his insistence on the immutability of his title, seems to find his actual grip on it quite slippery. He believes and does not believe his own argument, ready to assert it but unable to fight for it. Having already promised to negotiate with Bolingbroke, he asks Aumerle if he should 'send | Defiance to the traitor, and so die' instead, but the still-hopeful Aumerle now urges caution: 'let's fight with gentle words | Till time lend friends, and friends their helpful swords' (3.3.130–1). Though their positions would seem to be reversed from the previous scene, still it is only Aumerle who looks for ways to continue fighting; Richard only sees defiance as a quicker route to death. As Mowbray complained in the play's very first scene, words aren't enough; but Richard seems to have nothing else to offer in his own defence but stories of what could be, should be, has been. A sad story about the death of a king.

Much of the theatrical and critical reception of Richard and *Richard* has been shaped by just a few lines, delivered by Bolingbroke to Richard's favourites Bushy and Green before they are executed. In listing their crimes against Richard, and thus against the country, he says:

> You have, in manner, with your sinful hours
> Made a divorce betwixt his queen and him,
> Broke the possession of a royal bed,
> And stained the beauty of a fair queen's cheeks
> With tears, drawn from her eyes by your foul wrongs.
>
> (3.1.11–15)

These lines are all but impossible to interpret as anything but the most obvious suggestion: this divorce, this theft of Richard's bed, the Queen's tears, are meant to say that the Queen's place in the King's bed has been usurped by Bushy and Green—that his favourites are also his lovers. The mention of sin, stains, and 'foul wrongs' further emphasizes that Bolingbroke speaks of something more seriously aberrant than close friendship.

It is worth noting, of course, that Bolingbroke's description of a neglected and sorrowful Queen does not precisely match what we see—she seems to get along perfectly well with Bushy and Green in the single scene they share, and though she is frequently mournful, her sex life with Richard is never the stated cause, as it often is with other mournful wives in Shakespeare, including in the soon-to-be-written *Henry IV Part 1*. When the Queen and Richard part ways in Act 5, their language and behaviour are loving. And Bolingbroke is, of course, an enemy of Richard's and of the men against whom he makes this accusation. In the full context of the scene, these lines come from someone who is actively seeking to justify the deaths of the men about whom he speaks. It is possible we are not meant to take these lines seriously, and instead should see them as an example of the conventional kinds of slander used to discredit disliked favourites of a monarch. Editors Anthony Dawson and Paul Yachnin suggest this reading: 'But we recognize [. . .] the astutely political motivation behind the condemnation, as Bolingbroke clears the path toward the throne, shooting down Richard's confederates as proxies of the King.'[25] However, Bolingbroke's lines resonate, and have done throughout the play's history. The signs of Richard's failure to suit the norm are everywhere. Hinting that queerness is another way in which he is out of step with what he ought to do and ought to be simply, for many, feels right. Already he is a king without an heir. Already he is a king who will not fight. Already is a king whose friendships sit at the centre of his life.[26]

The twenty-first-century performance history of this play has often found ways to make Bolingbroke's implications true and directly

---

[25] *Richard II*, ed. Yachnin and Dawson, 74.
[26] Madhavi Menon's influential '*Richard II* and the Taint of Metonymy', *English Literary History* 70.3 (2003), 653–75, proposes that Richard's queerness is deeply embedded in the linguistic contest between himself and Bolingbroke.

expressed, including in the BBC's *Hollow Crown* TV series starring Ben Whishaw; the Royal Shakespeare Company's 2013 production with David Tennant in the title role; and the 2019 Shakespeare's Globe production in the indoor Sam Wanamaker Playhouse, also notable for being the first production of the play staged entirely by women of colour. Each of these productions depicted physical intimacy, usually kissing, between Richard and his favourites—generally not Bushy, Bagot, or Green, the actual subjects of Bolingbroke's accusation, but rather Richard's cousin Aumerle. These performances thus underscore a closeness that can be easier to overlook in the written text, but is a unique relationship both in the play overall and for Richard as a character.

In a world that is so shaped by the relationships between fathers and sons, by ties of blood, Richard lacks a living father to situate him within his family. Indeed, he can only be who he is *because* his father is dead. His title—and thus, his sense of self—entirely relies upon standing alone. Even without Bolingbroke's accusation, we can see that Richard chooses to surround himself with confidantes who are not the family members who so desperately wish to guide him. The one exception is Aumerle, the Duke of York's son, with whom he seems to share a particularly intimate relationship. Aumerle immediately flees to Richard's side when Richard returns from Ireland, and does not leave it until Richard is deposed. As Richard gives in to Bolingbroke, and once more to despair, Aumerle is overcome by emotion:

> Aumerle, thou weep'st, my tender-hearted cousin.
> We'll make foul weather with despisèd tears.
> Our sighs and they shall lodge the summer corn,
> And make a dearth in this revolting land.
> Or shall we play the wantons with our woes,
> And make some pretty match with shedding tears,
> As thus to drop them still upon one place
> Till they have fretted us a pair of graves
> Within the earth, and therein laid? 'There lies
> Two kinsmen digged their graves with weeping eyes.'
> (3.3.159–68)

Richard initially tries to imagine turning their tears towards revenge against the land and its people, but quickly pivots to an image that recalls his invocation in the previous scene to 'Make dust our paper, and with rainy eyes | Write sorrow on the bosom of the earth' (3.2.146–7). With tears the ink and the earth the paper, Richard reflexively imagines writing a chronicle of his sorrow into the land itself, this second time with Aumerle at his side. He is teasing, imagining it first as a kind of competition, but the sweet good humour is part of what makes the image so intimate. Even while waiting to descend to what he already knows will be some form of detainment and surely fears is the prelude to death, he pauses to try and make his crying companion smile with the image of the two of them united in grief, unparted in death.

In Act 4, in a mirror to the first scene's accusations, when Bolingbroke calls upon his and the murdered Gloucester's shared blood—'Which blood, like sacrificing Abel's cries, | Even from the tongueless caverns of the earth, | To me for justice and rough chastisement' (1.1.104–6)—it is Aumerle who is made the scapegoat. Gloucester's death is once again marshalled as an excuse for public accusation and an exchange of gages, symbols of a promise for a future duel, that—like so many things in Aumerle's life—takes a turn for the comic as gage after gage is thrown by a series of courtiers. Aumerle himself eventually runs out of gloves and has to ask to borrow one to throw at an accuser (4.1.83). His first opponent: Bagot, Richard's former fellow favourite. Echoes of the play's first scene ring in the accusers' deep sense of personal loyalty and duty—in Aumerle's case, especially in contrast to Bagot's defection. Bolingbroke sees himself as personally called to bring Gloucester justice; Aumerle is defiant in the face of accusations that would turn his service of Richard into a crime.

It's a curious prelude to the single scene that makes up the entire fourth act: Richard's deposition. By first directly recalling the play's first scene—now with the murder of Gloucester taken as a given, Richard's complicity unquestioned—Shakespeare establishes the altered world into which Richard is entering when he is summoned to openly give away his crown. As the accusations against Aumerle descend into a chaos that Bolingbroke cannot quite control—just as Richard could not help but transform the trial by combat into something else, something that placed himself at its centre—the deposition quickly slips out of Bolingbroke's hands and becomes Richard's tragedy to play. While words could not win Richard a war, now that they are the only tool remaining to him, he is newly ready to use what small power he has. Even if it cannot gain him back his crown, he is far better prepared than Bolingbroke to win a battle waged over the audience's attention and sympathy.[27]

What follows is a virtuosic performance, one that Bolingbroke observes with a sense of resigned weariness. Richard begins by refusing to straightforwardly observe the agreed-upon fiction that he has willingly given up his crown, and only grows more defiant from there. While Aumerle's defiance promised violence—'I have a thousand spirits in one breast | To answer twenty thousand such as you' (4.1.58–9)—Richard's comes in an altogether different key, one that his opponents seem to have no real idea how to combat. He takes pitiless advantage of their wrong-footedness, as when he calls for a conventional greeting shortly after he enters:

> God save the King! Will no man say, 'Amen'?
> Am I both priest and clerk? Well then, Amen.
> God save the King, although I be not he.
> And yet Amen, if heaven do think him me.
>
> (4.1.172–5)

This deliberate and yet sincere confusion lies at the heart of Richard's responses throughout the scene. His equation of the loss of his crown with a complete loss of identity serves to shake the confidence of Bolingbroke and his followers in the legitimacy of the scene they are staging: *does* God still think 'God save the King' refers to Richard? How can anyone know for sure? John Barton's production for the Royal Shakespeare Company in 1973 literalized this confusion by famously having two actors alternate the role of Richard on different nights, the play beginning with a silent prologue in which an actor dressed as Shakespeare selected which of the two would portray the king.

However, Richard also seems genuinely adrift in this sequence, the dramatic public performance of his feelings by no means meant to signal insincerity, though Bolingbroke and others sometimes seem to take it that way. But once again, that reaction is a case of Richard being misunderstood. Richard calls for a mirror so 'That it may show

[27] Isabel Karremann in *The Drama of Memory in Shakespeare's History Plays* (Cambridge: Cambridge University Press, 2015) reads this scene through the lens of another form of performance: coronation and beatification rituals.

me what a face I have, | Since it is bankrupt of his majesty' (4.1.265–6), and Bolingbroke readily obliges, but largely seems to be losing patience with Richard's histrionics.

RICHARD   A brittle glory shineth in this face.
    As brittle as the glory is the face,

    He shatters the glass

    For there it is, cracked in an hundred shivers.
    Mark, silent King, the moral of this sport:
    How soon my sorrow hath destroyed my face.

BOLINGBROKE   The shadow of your sorrow hath destroyed
    The shadow of your face.

(4.1.286–92)

But Richard simply cannot be bested in a battle of showmanship, and he maintains control to the end, 'beg[ging] one boon' of his cousin: to leave (4.1.301ff.). Bolingbroke orders him escorted to the Tower of London, a famous royal prison, but the power of the gesture has been pre-empted by Richard's request. Though he may now lack a crown and—perhaps—divine authority, Richard is even more effective than before at seizing control of any scene he enters.[28] As a subject, Bolingbroke's insistence on justice was too complicated for Richard to control; with the roles reversed, it is Richard who will not observe the script Bolingbroke has set out for him, and finds that it is sometimes easier to find power in defying authority than in asserting it. He finds himself most at ease in the place where, in some ways, he has always been: outside of expectations, outside of the norm, outside of kingship.

Theatre

Richard is never more powerful than when he has lost everything.[29] From the beginning of the play, he has marshalled pageantry and

---

[28] Katherine Eggert proposes in *Showing Like a Queen: Female Authority and Literary Experiment in Spenser, Shakespeare, and Milton* (Philadelphia: University of Pennsylvania Press, 2000) that such contests 'between who is fit to rule and who can most compellingly hold the stage' (79) are fundamental to the drama of the history plays overall.

[29] Donovan Sherman argues against 'the interpretive tradition that finds the theatricality of the un-kinged body a source of impotence' (23) in ' "What more remains?": Messianic Performance in *Richard II*', *Shakespeare Quarterly* 65.1 (2014), 22–48.

performance as his greatest weapons, sometimes to mixed success. But the less these acts of theatre serve as a mask for his divine, royal authority, the more potent they paradoxically become. Richard laments, 'I have no name, no title, | No, not that name was given me at the font, | But 'tis usurped. Alack the heavy day | That I have worn so many winters out | And know not now what name to call myself!' (4.1.254–8). And yet, unlike when he could confidently proclaim, 'Is not the King's name twenty thousand names? | Arm, arm, my name!' (3.2.85–6), he holds absolute sway over the proceedings. Never mind that said proceedings are his own deposition, what ought to be a ritual stripping of his power.[30] The onstage audience cannot find any way to force him to do their will—not to read a list of crimes, as Northumberland keeps insisting upon, nor to feel a sense of shame, as Bolingbroke's sarcastic retorts seem designed to provoke. In an encounter designed to symbolize Bolingbroke's assumption of authority and Richard's disgrace, Richard seizes the room's attention when he enters, then leaves it on his own terms.

Again and again, the play swings between the public displays that are the backbone of royal authority—or at least are meant to be—and the privacy of back halls and empty rooms. The former hints at the blurry line between monarchy and theatre, both reliant on the presence of an audience to uphold its power—something Richard, until his final scene, is never without. He is always observed, always forming and performing his identity for the benefit of the public. Who he is when he is not *seen* is as much the question as who he is when he does not have a title or a crown.

But Shakespeare's interest in probing the relationship between monarchy and theatre extends to the ostensibly private half of the divide as well. Behind closed doors, Shakespeare invites the audience to see themselves in his characters, placing us in the role of those who stand outside the halls of power, who can only know what they are told by the story's central players. Characters like the Queen, the Duchess of York, and even at times Richard himself are placed in the position of passive receivers of narrative, and used to reflect the vast world of

---

[30] In 'Magic Mirrors in *Richard II*', *Comparative Drama* 38.2–3 (2004), 151–81, Robert M. Schuler suggests Richard's three key moments of spectacle in this scene— holding the crown together, his self-deposition through reverse coronation, and calling for a mirror—are moments of 'magic', both in the sense of stage magic and as allusions to early modern beliefs about supernatural potential.

people who are buffeted by the tides of history rather than controlling them.

But despite this sense of powerlessness, these scenes demonstrate the power that the audience holds, which other spectators of history do not: the ability to see what should be unseen, to peek behind the doors and into the secret places where other characters cannot go. This is never more evident than in the play's only scene of extended soliloquy: Richard's prison cell.

When Richard is imprisoned and alone, he still has words to comfort him. Unlike Shakespeare's other famous Richard, Richard III, he seems only somewhat aware of the audience's presence, and not of the potential to win us as allies or turn us into enemies. He does not woo us, as some characters—villains especially—try to do. But even with no one but us to hear him, he still talks: 'I have been studying how I may compare | This prison where I live unto the world; | And for because the world is populous, | And here is not a creature but myself, | I cannot do it. Yet I'll hammer it out' (5.1.1–5). After a series of linguistic loops, he finds himself back where he started: alone. And yet, not alone, for we have heard it all. His monologue in some ways traces the shape of the play itself, expansive and then inexorably shrinking:

> Sometimes am I king;
> Then treasons make me wish myself a beggar,
> And so I am. Then crushing penury
> Persuades me I was better when a king;
> Then am I kinged again, and by and by,
> Think that I am unkinged by Bolingbroke,
> And straight am nothing.
>
> (5.5.32–8)

The narrowing of the spotlight back down to Richard himself, a man who thinks he is nothing, rather highlights how much space Richard fills. His little world is ours as well—'in one person, many people'— and he is the inescapable centre of gravity.

Richard seems to have discovered something new about himself in this period of silent contemplation, for when death comes for him, he does something we have never before seen him truly do: he fights back. 'Go thou, and fill another room in hell' (5.5.107) he cries as he kills a would-be murderer with the assassin's own blade, only to immediately be struck down himself. Richard's mind returns at the last to the connection between himself and the land, fashioning a curse for his murderer, Exton: 'That hand shall burn in never-quenching fire | That staggers thus my person. Exton, thy fierce hand | Hath with the King's blood stained the King's own land' (5.5.108–10). The erstwhile king and his land are divided at last—and yet, Richard imagines part of himself remaining to 'stain' the land that did not rise to aid him. To the last, he is devout in his belief in an unbreakable connection between himself and his country.

And, of course, this is a play, and thus death need not be the end. As Bolingbroke begins the play's final scene with a sequence of rhymed triumph—the capture and punishment of a series of would-be traitors—he is interrupted once again by unwelcome news, unwanted supplications. The intrusion of Richard's murder into Bolingbroke's finally calming court is the former king's ultimate theatrical coup, his last moment of scene-stealing. Though Bolingbroke may wear the crown, it is Richard who will irrevocably define his reign, the stain of his blood indelible, and as impossible to ignore as the presence of his coffin in the throne room. Though his body goes unseen, Shakespeare ensures that Richard is permitted to appear in person one last time, one final confrontation with his rival. Shakespeare makes Richard's death an embodied presence, a physical fact in the form of this coffin. It is a last chance to use the power of the theatre to triumph where by any practical measure he has failed: in death, he guarantees that his name will not and cannot be forgotten.

Richard II is a play both large and small. The story of a man, and the story of a kingdom. The story of a family, and the story of a dynasty. Like most of Shakespeare's plays, it can be read in a hundred different ways—certainly in far more than the few lenses provided here. And it can be read as a story on its own merits, not only as a tiny snipping of a vast tapestry of history that surrounds its central players. It is a play that asks—shamelessly contradictory, as Shakespeare is at his best—whether it is truly possible to untether oneself from the past, to be unmoored from family and the history they carry, to stand alone; it also asks what happens if one always looks backwards and inwards, to sad stories of the death of kings rather than to the present, impending threat of the here and now. Its histories on the page, on the stage, and in the culture are rich and interesting—but it is, in the end, a story that once was new.

NOTE ON THE TEXT

Richard II was entered in the Stationers' Register on 29 August 1597 to Andrew Wise, who issued the first quarto, printed by Valentine Simmes, later the same year. The title page calls it a 'Tragedie'. Two reprints of 1598 testify to the play's popularity. On 25 June 1603, entitlement was transferred from Wise to Matthew Law, who published two additional quartos in 1608 and 1615. A further edition appeared in 1634. In the 1623 Folio, the play is placed according to the chronology of events in the Histories section, after the chronological outlier *King John*. Its title is changed to 'The life and death of King Richard the Second', in line with 'The life and death of King Iohn' before it.

The first quarto is on the whole reliable, but the absolutely crucial deposition episode (4.1.154–319) is missing, probably due to political censorship. This passage first appeared in the quarto of 1608, and then in fuller form in the Folio. The Folio also adds act and scene divisions for the first time, provides different and more ample stage directions, introduces variant readings which probably include minor revisions by Shakespeare, cuts a few lines, corrects some of the errors accrued in the quarto reprints, and removes some of the profanity, typically by replacing 'God' with 'heauen'. These changes indicate the influence of a manuscript source that was markedly different from the printer's copy for the first edition. The act divisions reflect the practices of Jacobean indoor theatres, and the removal of profanity responds to legislation of 1606 forbidding profanity on stage. The manuscript therefore probably came from the theatre.

The Folio text was not, however, printed from this manuscript. Instead, readings from the manuscript were annotated into a copy of the third quarto of 1598 (supplemented with a few pages of the 1615 edition). The efficiency of the annotator fluctuated, but—judging from the Folio's correction of errors introduced in quarto reprints—on average about half the variants in the manuscript were captured by this process.

The Folio is a modified reprint that perpetuates many errors from the quartos; as a text of a different version of the play, it is limited by the annotator's failure to transfer many of the manuscript's readings.

Any authorial revision was light. The Folio's leading characteristics are conflicting: it restores a passage that belonged in the play as Shakespeare originally wrote it, and it reflects some but not all the features of the play as it existed at a later stage in its development, including a different form of censorship.

This edition, like others, opts for the first quarto as copy text, on account of its greater proximity to Shakespeare's writing and to the early performances on stage. However, the censored deposition episode is restored from the Folio. The Folio's onward authorial and theatrical revisions (as well as its errors) are rejected. This preserves the copy-text version, and avoids a merely partial representation of the manuscript behind the Folio.

John Jowett

SELECT BIBLIOGRAPHY

The Oxford World's Classics depend on the extraordinary editorial labours of the *New Oxford Shakespeare* team, who, under the leadership of Gary Taylor, John Jowett, Terri Bourus, and Gabriel Egan, have rethought details large and small about these texts. Readers are encouraged to explore the resources of that edition, and to refer to *The New Oxford Shakespeare: Modern Critical Edition* (Oxford: Oxford University Press, 2016) for further information. All references to other works by Shakespeare in the introduction and notes to this edition are taken from the *New Oxford Shakespeare*.

General Reading

De Grazia, Margreta, and Stanley Wells, eds, *The New Cambridge Companion to Shakespeare* (Cambridge: Cambridge University Press, 2010).

Gajowski, Evelyn, ed., *The Arden Research Handbook of Contemporary Shakespeare Criticism* (London: Bloomsbury, 2022).

Karim-Cooper, Farah, *The Great White Bard: How to Love Shakespeare while Talking about Race* (London: Simon and Schuster, 2023).

McEvoy, Sean, *Shakespeare: The Basics* (London: Taylor and Francis, 2006).

Orlin, Lena Cowen, *The Private Life of William Shakespeare* (Oxford: Oxford University Press, 2021).

Smith, Emma, *This Is Shakespeare* (London: Pelican, 2019).

Smuts, Malcolm, ed., *The Oxford Handbook of the Age of Shakespeare* (Oxford: Oxford University Press, 2018).

On Richard II

Archer, John Michael, 'Fruits of Duty: Honor in Shakespeare's *King Richard II*', *Modern Language Notes*, 135.5 (2020), 1170–83.

Baldo, Jonathan, *Memory in Shakespeare's Histories: Stages of Forgetting* (London: Routledge, 2011).

Bergeron, David, 'The Deposition Scene in *Richard II*', *Renaissance Papers 1974* (1975), 31–7.

Brown, Judith, 'Pretty Richard (in Three Parts)', in Madhavi Menon, ed., *Shakesqueer* (Durham, NC: Duke University Press, 2011), 286–93.

Clegg, Cyndia Susan, ' "By the choise and intimation of all the realme": *Richard II* and Elizabethan Press Censorship', *Shakespeare Quarterly* 48.1 (1997), 432–48.

Garber, Marjorie, 'Richard II', in *Shakespeare After All* (New York: Random House, 2004), 238–69.

Hammer, Paul E. J., 'Shakespeare's *Richard II*, the Play of 7 February 1601, and the Essex Rising', *Shakespeare Quarterly* 15.9 (2008), 1–35.

Hopkins, Lisa, 'The King's Melting Body: *Richard II*', in Richard Dutton and Jean E. Howard, eds, *A Companion to Shakespeare: The Histories* (Blackwell: Oxford, 2003), 395–411.

Howard, Jean E. and Phyllis Rackin, *Engendering a Nation* (London: Routledge, 1997).

Karreman, Isabel, *The Drama of Memory in Shakespeare's History Plays* (Cambridge: Cambridge University Press, 2015).

Kurtz, Martha A., ' "Mock not": The Problem of Laughter in *Richard II*', *University of Toronto Quarterly* 65.4 (1996), 584–99.

Luis-Martínez, Zenón, 'Shakespeare's Historical Drama as *Traurspiel: Richard II*—And After', *English Literary History* 75.3 (2008), 673–705.

McMillan, Scott, 'Shakespeare's *Richard II:* Eyes of Sorrow, Eyes of Desire', *Shakespeare Quarterly* 35.1 (1985), 40–52.

Menon, Madhavi, '*Richard II* and the Taint of Metonymy', *English Literary History* 70.3 (2003), 653–75.

Rosenfeld, Colleen Ruth, 'The Queen's Conceit in *Richard II*', *Studies in English Literature* 60.1 (2020), 25–46.

Sherman, Donovan, ' "What more remains?": Messianic Performance in *Richard II*', *Shakespeare Quarterly* 65.1 (2014), 22–48.

Smith, Molly, 'Minor Scenes and "Mutant" Conflicts in *Richard II*', in Dympna Callaghan, ed., *A Feminist Companion to Shakespeare* (Malden: Blackwell, 2016), 281–93.

Zitner, Sheldon P., 'Aumerle's Conspiracy', *Studies in English Literature* 14 (1974), 239–57.

A CHRONOLOGY OF
WILLIAM SHAKESPEARE

1564   (26 Apr.) William Shakespeare, third child of John Shakespeare (a glover) and Mary Arden, is baptized.

1569   Shakespeare probably attends King's New School.

         Northern Rebellion.

1582   (27–8 Nov.) Shakespeare, still a minor, and Anne Hathaway, pregnant, file for a marriage licence.

1583   (26 May) First child, Susanna, is christened.

1584   First attempted English settlement in America (Roanoke).

1585   (2 Feb.) Hamnet and Judith, twins, are christened.

c.1587   *The Two Gentlemen of Verona* likely written. An earlier draft may have been performed in Stratford-upon-Avon, and some elements may have been revised mid-1590s.

1587   *Holinshed's Chronicles* (2nd edition), source for Shakespeare's history plays.

1588   (Aug.) Defeat of Spanish Armada.

c.1592   Shakespeare moves to London some time before 1592. *Groatsworth of Wit* (Robert Greene, 1592) contains the thinly veiled first reference to Shakespeare on the theatrical scene ('an upstart crow'), and alludes to *Henry VI, Part III* ('tiger's heart wrapped in a players hide'). Contains potential allusions to plagiarism, and attacks him for his actor credentials.

         Henry VI, Part I is performed by Lord Strange's Men. Shakespeare identified as author of 2.4, 4.2, and parts of 4.3–4.5, probably later additions (maybe added 1594–5). Also includes work by Nashe and Marlowe.

         Likely composition date of *Edward III*. Though published anonymously, attribution scholars suggest Shakespeare wrote part of scenes 2, 3, and 12.

1592   *Arden of Faversham* first published (anonymously). Many critics agree Shakespeare had a hand in scenes 4–8, and dispute scene 9.

Playhouses are shut for the plague, opening for a short season in Dec. 1593–Feb. 1594, closing again after that.

1592-3   Likely composition of *Sir Thomas More*, originally written by Munday and Chettle. It was revised by several writers, probably around 1603–4, including a three-page handwritten revision attributed to Shakespeare.

1593   (18 Apr.) *Venus and Adonis* is registered in the Stationers' Register. Printed as a quarto, and relatively free of errors, it suggests the competence of printer Richard Field.

1594   Short version of *Henry VI, Part II*, 'The first part of the Contention of the Two Famous Houses of York and Lancaster, with the Death of the good Duke Humphrey', is published. Authorship contested: Shakespeare securely identified as the author of Act 3 and Young Clifford's speech.

          The Taming of a Shrew, a text with radical differences from *The Taming of the Shrew*, is printed. The familiar version would not be printed until 1623.

          (6 Feb.) *Titus Andronicus* is registered with the Stationers' Register. On 24 Jan., Henslowe records the performance of the play by Sussex's Men as 'new'. New can, however, mean recently licensed or republished: it was likely written between 1584 and 1594.

          (9 May) *The Ravishment of Lucrece* is registered in the Stationers' Register, printed by Field. It is dedicated to the Earl of Southampton, Shakespeare's patron.

          (Summer) Lord Chamberlain's Men formed.

          (28 Dec.) *The Comedy of Errors* is performed at Gray's Inn, to tumult and disorder. Becomes known as the Night of Errors.

1595   Likely date of composition of *Richard II*.

          Henry VI, Part III (which was created by 1592) is printed as an octavo, titled 'The True Tragedie of Richard Duke of York, and the Death of Good King Henrie the Sixt'.

1596   Thomas Lodge recalls an early *Hamlet*, in which the lines 'Hamlet, revenge!' feature.

          First edition of *Edward III*, which had 'been sundry times played about the City of London'.

          Likely composition date of *King John*.

(11 Aug.) Hamnet dies aged 11, and is buried in the churchyard of Holy Trinity, Stratford.

*c.*1597   Francis Mere's *Palladis Tamia*, 'Wit's Treasury. Being the Second Part of Wit's Common Wealth', references twelve plays as belonging to Shakespeare: *Gentlemen of Verona*, *Comedy of Errors*, *Love's Labour's Lost*, *Love's Labour Won*, *A Midsummer Night's Dream*, *Merchant of Venice*, *Richard II* & *III*, *Henry IV*, *King John*, *Titus Andronicus*, and *Romeo and Juliet*.

1597   *Romeo and Juliet* published.

Shakespeare buys a house on 'New Place', on Chapel Street, the second largest in Stratford.

Richard II first appears as a quarto edition.

Richard III is published in a quarto.

(13 Apr.) James Burbage's lease on the Theatre expires, and he purchases Blackfriars' Monastery. However, the aristocratic residents of the area complain to the Privy Council, preventing the company from moving in.

(July) After a salacious performance at the Swan, the Privy Council assents to the Lord Mayor and Alderman's petition for the surpressing of stage plays, and further orders the dismantling of Shoreditch and Bankside theatres, including the Theatre. However, this is not final, and the Theatre ends up reopening.

James Burbage dies.

(Christmas period) *Love's Labour's Lost*, and two other plays, are performed before Queen Elizabeth. The company is paid £40.

1598   Second Quarto of *Richard II* and *III* published, now bearing Shakespeare's name. *Love's Labour's Lost* is also published 'by W. Shakespere'—first extant copy, but self-described as 'Newly Corrected and Augmented'.

Henry IV, Part I is newly published in quarto, printed with 'Falstaff' rather than 'Oldcastle', under pressure from the Cobham family, descendants of the historical Oldcastle.

(28 Dec.) Unable to secure a lease with the landlord of the Theatre, Giles Allen and the Burbage brothers, along with a team of builders, disassemble the Theatre under the cover of darkness, ship the timber across to Bankside, and erect the Globe.

1598–9   (Christmas period) The Chamberlain's Men play twice in court.

1599   (21 Feb.) Globe agreement drawn up as a tripartite lease, with Shakespeare, as part of the Chamberlain's Men, owning 1/10th of the shares.

(*c*. Feb.) 'To the Queen', composed for a court performance, written. Stylometric evidence suggests it is Shakespeare's work.

(Mar.) Essex leaves for Ireland with 16,000 troops, returning in Sept., a failure.

Second, longer (still anonymous) version of *Romeo and Juliet* is published with a title-page claiming that it is 'Newly corrected, augmented, amended'.

Likely composition date of *Julius Caesar*.

Third edition of *Henry IV, Part I* is published, including Shakespeare's name for the first time.

The Passionate Pilgrim (two editions) is published as a pamphlet in octavo format. The title-page attributes the work to Shakespeare, though only five poems can be certainly attributed to him. Five of the poems would later appear in Shakespeare's *Sonnets* (138 and 144) and *Love's Labour's Lost*. It includes poems by Richard Barnfield, Thomas Deloney, Christopher Marlowe, Walter Raleigh, and Bartholomew Griffin.

1599–1600   Chamberlain's Men perform twice at court over the Christmas period.

1600   *The Merchant of Venice* first published.

First quarto of *Much Ado About Nothing*.

Likely date of composition of *As You Like It*.

Likely date of composition of *The Merry Wives of Windsor*.

A Midsummer's Night's Dream is printed in quarto.

Henry IV, Part II is printed in quarto.

Henry V is printed in quarto, as a corrupted shortened text.

1600–1   Chamberlain's Men perform twice at court over the Christmas period.

1601   (7 Feb.) On the evening of the Essex Rebellion, supporters of the Earl of Essex request a performance of *Richard II*. The Lord Chamberlain's Men brought in for questioning by the Privy Council.

(8 Feb.) Essex rebellion. The Earl of Essex makes a bid for power, marching on court (unsuccessfully), before marching back through the city, barricading himself in Essex House, and finally surrendering. Southampton, Shakespeare's patron, escapes with imprisonment.

(8 Sept.) John Shakespeare buried, the house on Henley Street passing on to William Shakespeare.

Probable date of composition of *Twelfth Night*. John Manningham attends a performance of the play at the Middle Temple on the Feast of Candlemas, 1602.

1601–2   Chamberlain's Men perform three times at court over the Christmas period.

1602   *Sir John Falstaff and The Merry Wives of Windsor* is first printed in quarto.

The intent to publish 'The Tragicall Historie of Hamlet Prince of Denmarke' is entered in the Stationers' Register, though the 'first quarto' will not be printed until autumn 1603.

1603   Date of printing of *Hamlet* first quarto (earliest extant copy).

(2 Feb.) Chamberlain's Men play for the last time before the queen.

(7 Feb.) *Troilus and Cressida* entered in the Stationers' Register, likely composed 1602. It is not, however, printed until 1609.

(24 Mar.) Queen dies and her 'kinsman, the King of Scots' James VI / I ascends to the throne.

(17 May) Troupe becomes the King's Men.

1604   (Jan.) Private production of *Love's Labour's Lost* staged by the King's Men, at Southampton or Cecil House.

Likely composition of *Othello*, originally titled *The Moor of Venice*.

(1 Nov.) *Othello* (stage name 'The Moor of Venice') first performed at court on Hallowmas Day.

(26 Dec.) *Measure for Measure* performed in front of the new king and court at the Banqueting House at Whitehall.

(28 Dec.) *The Comedy of Errors* performed for King James.

1604–5   Printing of second, longer quarto of *Hamlet*, over the New Year (hence, some dated 1604 (3 copies), others 1605 (4 copies)).

1605   *All's Well That Ends Well* probable composition date. Adapted by Middleton most likely around 1621. First recorded performance 1741.

        (Feb.) *The Merchant of Venice* performed at court twice in three days.

1606   Most likely composition date of *Timon of Athens*.

        Original composition date of *Macbeth*. Adapted a decade later with Thomas Middleton. May have been staged at the court of James I as well as the Globe.

        (26 Dec.) Shakespeare's *King Lear* performed at court.

        Master of Revels now able to license plays for print.

        Likely date of composition of *Antony and Cleopatra*; first performed around 1607.

1607   Virginia Company, chartered by 1606, founds Jamestown colony.

        (26 Nov.) *King Lear* entered on the Stationers' Register. The First Quarto printed 1608, giving the longest and earliest text.

1608   New edition of *Richard II* includes new deposition scene.

        The King's Men reassume the lease of Blackfriars from Henry Evans.

        Mary Arden, Shakespeare's mother, dies.

        Likely composition of *Coriolanus*. There were no recorded performances during Shakespeare's lifetime. However, possible allusions can be found in *c.*1609 by Robert Armin and Ben Jonson. The first confirmed performance was Nahum Tate's 1681 adaptation.

1609   *Pericles* is first published (likely written around 1608), and reprinted frequently. First edition is very corrupted. First eleven scenes likely written by George Wilkins.

        (28 Jan.) *Troilus and Cressida* is published under unusual circumstances, as a 'new play' 'never staled with the stage, never clapper-clawed by the hands of the vulgar'. It was likely only new to readers. It was originally submitted to the Stationers' Register six years prior, but it was never published. In 1609, Bonian and Walley entered it on the register as written by William Shakespeare and acted by His Majesty's Servants at the Globe.

Thomas Thorpe publishes a quarto edition of the *Sonnets*. Some had circulated since at least 1599 in *The Passionate Pilgrim*.

King's Men assume operations at Blackfriars, primarily using it as their winter theatre.

1610	Likely composition of *Cymbeline*.
c.1609/11	Likely composition of *The Winter's Tale*.
1611	Likely composition of *The Tempest*, the last play Shakespeare composed alone.

Simon Forman describes seeing *Macbeth* (20 Apr.), and *The Winter's Tale* (15 May) at the Globe, and also *Cymbeline* (no date or theatre listed).

1612   (May) Shakespeare gives evidence at the Court of Requests, in London.

Likely date of *Henry VIII* ('All is True') composition, with Fletcher. Shakespeare would also collaborate with Fletcher on *Cardenio* and his likely final play, *The Two Noble Kinsmen*.

1613   (Feb.) King's Men perform at Whitehall for the nuptials of Princess Elizabeth and Prince Frederick, performing fourteen plays including *Much Ado About Nothing*, *Othello*, *The Winter's Tale*, and *The Tempest*. Paid £93 6s. 8d.

(Mar.) Shakespeare buys a home in the Blackfriars' Constituency, London, for £140. At some point between 1610 and 1613, however, Shakespeare has moved back to Stratford.

(29 Jun.) *Henry VIII* performed at the Globe, probably written *c*.1612. During the performance, and as noted by Sir Henry Wotton, a theatrical cannon misfired and caught the thatch. Within a year a new Globe, with a tiled roof, was built on the same site.

1613–14   Likely date of composition of *The Two Noble Kinsmen*, probably written with Fletcher.

1616   (25 Mar.) Shakespeare summons his lawyer, Francis Collins, and makes his last Will and Testament. The will was possibly drafted in Jan., and revised in Mar. to reflect Judith's marital status. The will is typical of a Jacobean man of means, although it is light on philanthropy.

(23 Apr.) Shakespeare dies, aged 52. He is buried at Holy Trinity Church, Stratford-upon-Avon.

1618   (Easter Monday) Performance of *Twelfth Night* at court.

1622   *The Tragedy of Othello* printed in quarto (as a shorter text). Claims that Shakespeare's 'name is enough' to sell any play.

1623   The First Folio, 'Comedies, Histories, & Tragedies', a collection of thirty-six plays, is published. Compiled by Shakespeare's fellow actors and friends John Heminges and Henry Condell.

1634   Publication of quarto text of *The Two Noble Kinsmen*, attributed to Shakespeare and John Fletcher on the title-page.

THE TRAGEDY OF KING
RICHARD THE SECOND

THE ROLES IN THE PLAY

KING RICHARD II
The QUEEN, his wife
GAUNT, Duke of Lancaster, Richard's uncle
Harry BOLINGBROKE, Duke of Hereford, John of Gaunt's son,
    later KING HENRY IV
DUCHESS OF GLOUCESTER, widow of Gaunt's and York's brother
Duke of YORK, King Richard's uncle
DUCHESS OF YORK
Duke of AUMERLE, their son
Thomas MOWBRAY, Duke of Norfolk

Favourites of King Richard
GREEN
BAGOT
BUSHY

Of Bolingbroke's Party
Percy, Earl of NORTHUMBERLAND
HARRY PERCY, his son
Lord ROSS
Lord WILLOUGHBY

Of King Richard's Party
Earl of SALISBURY
BISHOP OF CARLISLE
Sir Stephen SCROPE

Lord BERKELEY
Lord FITZWALTER
Duke of SURREY
ABBOT OF WESTMINSTER
Sir Piers EXTON
LORD MARSHAL
HERALDS

CAPTAIN of the Welsh army
LADIES attending the Queen
GARDENER
Gardener's MEN
Exton's MEN
KEEPER of the prison at Pomfret
GROOM of King Richard's stable

Lords, soldiers, servingmen, attendants

RICHARD II

Sc. 1   *Enter King Richard [and] John of Gaunt, with [the Lord Marshal,] other nobles, and attendants*

KING RICHARD   Old John of Gaunt, time-honoured Lancaster,
Hast thou according to thy oath and bond
Brought hither Henry Hereford, thy bold son,
Here to make good the boist'rous late appeal,
Which then our leisure would not let us hear,   5
Against the Duke of Norfolk, Thomas Mowbray?

GAUNT   I have, my liege.

KING RICHARD   Tell me moreover, hast thou sounded him
If he appeal the Duke on ancient malice,
Or worthily, as a good subject should,   10
On some known ground of treachery in him?

GAUNT   As near as I could sift him on that argument,
On some apparent danger seen in him
Aimed at your highness, no inveterate malice.

KING RICHARD   Then call them to our presence.   15
                    [Exit one or more attendants]
                                            Face to face,
And frowning brow to brow, ourselves will hear
The accuser and the accusèd freely speak.
High-stomached are they both and full of ire;
In rage, deaf as the sea, hasty as fire.

Enter Bolingbroke Duke of Hereford, and Mowbray Duke of Norfolk

---

Sc. 1 1.1.0 **John of Gaunt** (named after Gaunt—i.e. Ghent—his birthplace; his title was Duke of Lancaster)
1.1.3 **Hereford** (pronounced as two syllables or with lightly sounded medial *e*)
1.1.4 **boist'rous** rough, violent
1.1.4 **late appeal** recent accusation
1.1.5 **leisure** i.e. lack of leisure
1.1.9 **appeal** accuse
1.1.9 **on ancient malice** out of long-standing enmity

1.1.12 **As near** so far
1.1.12 **sift** discover by questioning
1.1.12 **argument** subject
1.1.13 **apparent** evident
1.1.15 **presence** (alternatively punctuated, with *Face to face...brow to brow* qualifying *them*)
1.1.16 **ourselves** we ourselves (the royal plural)
1.1.18 **High-stomached** proud, stubborn
1.1.19 **deaf** i.e. as unheeding of pleas

BOLINGBROKE   Many years of happy days befall   20
  My gracious sovereign, my most loving liege!

MOWBRAY   Each day still better others' happiness,
  Until the heavens, envying earth's good hap,
  Add an immortal title to your crown!

KING RICHARD   We thank you both. Yet one but flatters us,   25
  As well appeareth by the cause you come,
  Namely, to appeal each other of high treason.
  Cousin of Hereford, what dost thou object
  Against the Duke of Norfolk, Thomas Mowbray?

BOLINGBROKE   First—heaven be the record to my speech—   30
  In the devotion of a subject's love,
  Tend'ring the precious safety of my Prince,
  And free from other misbegotten hate,
  Come I appellant to this princely presence.
  Now, Thomas Mowbray, do I turn to thee;   35
  And mark my greeting well, for what I speak
  My body shall make good upon this earth,
  Or my divine soul answer it in heaven.
  Thou art a traitor and a miscreant,
  Too good to be so, and too bad to live,   40
  Since the more fair and crystal is the sky,
  The uglier seem the clouds that in it fly.
  Once more, the more to aggravate the note,
  With a foul traitor's name stuff I thy throat,
  And wish, so please my sovereign, ere I move,   45
  What my tongue speaks my right-drawn sword may prove.

MOWBRAY   Let not my cold words here accuse my zeal.
  'Tis not the trial of a woman's war,
  The bitter clamour of two eager tongues,
  Can arbitrate this cause betwixt us twain.   50

1.1.22 **still** continually
1.1.23 **hap** fortune
1.1.24 **immortal title** i.e. eternal life
  (the *crown* being an earthly *title*)
1.1.28 **object** charge
1.1.32 **Tend'ring** having care for
1.1.34 **appellant** as accuser
1.1.36 **greeting** address
1.1.38 **divine** immortal

1.1.40 **good** socially high-ranking
1.1.43 **aggravate** add weight to
1.1.46 **right-drawn** drawn in a just cause
1.1.47 **accuse my zeal** impugn my
  ardour
1.1.49 **eager** sharp, impetuous
1.1.50 **arbitrate** decide (without implying
  compromise)
1.1.50 **cause** case, dispute

The blood is hot that must be cooled for this.
Yet can I not of such tame patience boast
As to be hushed and naught at all to say.
First, the fair reverence of your highness curbs me
From giving reins and spurs to my free speech,   55
Which else would post until it had returned
These terms of treason doubled down his throat.
Setting aside his high blood's royalty,
And let him be no kinsman to my liege,
I do defy him, and I spit at him,   60
Call him a slanderous coward and a villain;
Which to maintain, I would allow him odds,
And meet him, were I tied to run afoot
Even to the frozen ridges of the Alps,
Or any other ground inhabitable,   65
Wherever Englishman durst set his foot.
Meantime, let this defend my loyalty:
By all my hopes, most falsely doth he lie.

BOLINGBROKE [*throwing down his gage*]
Pale trembling coward, there I throw my gage,
Disclaiming here the kindred of the King,   70
And lay aside my high blood's royalty,
Which fear, not reverence, makes thee to except.
If guilty dread have left thee so much strength
As to take up mine honour's pawn, then stoop.
By that, and all the rites of knighthood else,   75
Will I make good against thee, arm to arm,
What I have spoke or thou canst worse devise.

MOWBRAY [*taking up the gage*]   I take it up, and by that sword
          I swear

1.1.51 **The blood** (of Bolingbroke)
1.1.51 **cooled** (in death)
1.1.56 **post** ride with speed
1.1.59 **let him be** as if he were
1.1.62 **maintain** uphold in battle
1.1.63 **tied** obliged
1.1.65 **inhabitable** uninhabitable
1.1.67 **this** (the following
        declaration, or possibly
        his sword)

1.1.68.1 *gage* the pledge of a challenge;
        probably a glove or possibly a mail coif,
        a detachable hood made of chain-mail
        and used as armour
1.1.70 **kindred** i.e. the privileges of
        kinship with
1.1.72 **except** set aside
1.1.74 **pawn** pledge
1.1.78 **I take it up** (thereby accepting the
        challenge)

Which gently laid my knighthood on my shoulder,
I'll answer thee in any fair degree, 80
Or chivalrous design of knightly trial;
And when I mount, alive may I not light
If I be traitor or unjustly fight!

KING RICHARD [*to Bolingbroke*] What doth our cousin lay to
    Mowbray's charge?
  It must be great that can inherit us 85
  So much as of a thought of ill in him.

BOLINGBROKE   Look what I speak, my life shall prove it true:
That Mowbray hath received eight thousand nobles
In name of lendings for your highness's soldiers,
The which he hath detained for lewd employments, 90
Like a false traitor and injurious villain.
Besides I say, and will in battle prove,
Or here or elsewhere to the furthest verge
That ever was surveyed by English eye,
That all the treasons for these eighteen years 95
Complotted and contrivèd in this land
Fetch from false Mowbray their first head and spring.
Further I say, and further will maintain
Upon his bad life to make all this good,
That he did plot the Duke of Gloucester's death, 100
Suggest his soon-believing adversaries,
And consequently, like a traitor-coward,
Sluiced out his innocent soul through streams of blood;

1.1.79 **gently** nobly, generously
1.1.80 **degree** way, manner
1.1.81 **chivalrous...trial** knightly combat of a kind allowed by the laws of chivalry
1.1.82 **light** alight
1.1.85 **inherit us** put us in possession
1.1.87 **Look what** whatever
1.1.88 **nobles** gold coins
1.1.89 **In name of lendings** as advances on pay (such as were made when regular pay could not be given)
1.1.90 **lewd employments** improper use
1.1.91 **injurious** insolently malicious
1.1.93 **Or** either
1.1.96 **Complotted** plotted with others

1.1.97 **Fetch** have as their source
1.1.97 **head** source (as of a river)
1.1.98–9 **maintain | Upon** uphold my accusations against (by implication, by ending *his bad life*)
1.1.100 **Gloucester's death** (The Duke of Gloucester was murdered under doubtful circumstances. Richard appears to have instigated it, and Mowbray to have direct responsibility.)
1.1.101 **Suggest** insinuate falsehoods to
1.1.101 **his...adversaries** (This implicates Richard himself.)
1.1.101 **soon-believing** credulous
1.1.102 **consequently** subsequently
1.1.103 **Sluiced** made flow

Which blood, like sacrificing Abel's cries,
Even from the tongueless caverns of the earth, 105
To me for justice and rough chastisement:
And, by the glorious worth of my descent,
This arm shall do it, or this life be spent.

KING RICHARD   How high a pitch his resolution soars!
Thomas of Norfolk, what sayst thou to this? 110

MOWBRAY   O, let my sovereign turn away his face,
And bid his ears a little while be deaf,
Till I have told this slander of his blood
How God and good men hate so foul a liar!

KING RICHARD   Mowbray, impartial are our eyes and ears. 115
Were he my brother, nay, my kingdom's heir,
As he is but my father's brother's son,
Now by my sceptre's awe I make a vow
Such neighbour-nearness to our sacred blood
Should nothing privilege him nor partialize 120
The unstooping firmness of my upright soul.
He is our subject, Mowbray, so art thou,
Free speech and fearless I to thee allow.

MOWBRAY   Then, Bolingbroke, as low as to thy heart
Through the false passage of thy throat thou liest! 125
Three parts of that receipt I had for Cálais,
Disbursed I duly to his highness' soldiers.
The other part reserved I by consent,
For that my sovereign liege was in my debt,
Upon remainder of a dear account 130
Since last I went to France to fetch his queen.

1.1.104–5 **Which...earth** The image is
from Genesis 4:10.
1.1.104 **sacrificing Abel's** (alludes to
Genesis 4:4)
1.1.106 **chastisement** (accented on the
first and third syllables)
1.1.109 **pitch** highest point to which
a falcon soars before stooping
1.1.113 **slander of his blood** reproach,
disgrace to his royal ancestry (or 'to his
own honour')

1.1.114 **God and good men** (a proverbial
phrase)
1.1.120 **privilege** (pronounced as two
syllables)
1.1.120 **partialize** render partial
1.1.126 **Three...had** three-quarters of the
sum received
1.1.130 **Upon...account** for the balance of
a large sum of money
1.1.131 **fetch his queen** negotiated the
marriage and accompanied the French
princess to England

Now swallow down that lie. For Gloucester's death,
I slew him not, but to my own disgrace
Neglected my sworn duty in that case.
For you my noble lord of Lancaster,   135
The honourable father to my foe,
Once did I lay an ambush for your life,
A trespass that doth vex my grievèd soul;
But ere I last received the sacrament
I did confess it, and exactly begged   140
Your grace's pardon, and I hope I had it.
This is my fault. As for the rest appealed
It issues from the rancour of a villain,
A recreant and most degenerate traitor,
Which in myself I boldly will defend,   145

    [*He throws down his gage*]

And interchangeably hurl down my gage
Upon this overweening traitor's foot,
To prove myself a loyal gentleman
Even in the best blood chambered in his bosom;
In haste whereof most heartily I pray   150
Your highness to assign our trial day.

    [*Bolingbroke takes up the gage*]

KING RICHARD   Wrath-kindled gentlemen, be ruled by me,.
Let's purge this choler without letting blood.
This we prescribe, though no physician:
Deep malice makes too deep incisïon;   155

1.1.132, 135 **For** as for
1.1.134 **my sworn duty** i.e. to Richard
    (It is implied here, and less ambiguously
    elsewhere (e.g. 1.2.37–9, 2.2.102), that
    Richard ordered Mowbray to kill
    Gloucester.)
1.1.138 **vex** grieve, afflict
1.1.140 **exactly** expressly, fully
1.1.142 **appealed** accused
1.1.144 **recreant** (could be either adjective
    or noun)
1.1.145 **in myself** in my own person
    (i.e. in battle)
1.1.146 **interchangeably** reciprocally,
    in turn

1.1.149 **Even in** i.e. to the extent of
    shedding
1.1.149 **chambered** enclosed
1.1.150 **In haste whereof** to hasten which
1.1.153 **purge** expel (by prohibiting
    purgatives)
1.1.153 **choler** bile, anger (viewed as sickness)
1.1.153 **letting blood** (in combat; as was
    practised by physicians to draw disease
    from the body)
1.1.154 **physician** (four syllables; as in
    incisïon, l. 1.1.155)
1.1.155 **malice** enmity; virulence (of a disease)
1.1.155 **makes** (on the surgical analogy,
    'requires')

Forget, forgive, conclude, and be agreed;
Our doctors say this is no month to bleed.
Good uncle, let this end where it begun.
We'll calm the Duke of Norfolk, you your son.

GAUNT   To be a make-peace shall become my age.   160
Throw down, my son, the Duke of Norfolk's gage.

KING RICHARD   And Norfolk, throw down his.

GAUNT   When, Harry, when?
Obedience bids I should not bid again.

KING RICHARD   Norfolk, throw down! We bid; there is no boot.

MOWBRAY   Myself I throw, dread sovereign, at thy foot.   165
My life thou shalt command, but not my shame.
The one my duty owes, but my fair name,
Despite of death that lives upon my grave,
To dark dishonour's use thou shalt not have.
I am disgraced, impeached, and baffled here,   170
Pierced to the soul with slander's venomed spear,
The which no balm can cure but his heart blood
Which breathed this poison.

KING RICHARD   Rage must be withstood.
Give me his gage. Lions make leopards tame.

MOWBRAY   Yea, but not change his spots. Take but my shame,   175
And I resign my gage. My dear, dear lord,
The purest treasure mortal times afford

1.1.157 **doctors** (probably 'leaned men, astrologers')

1.1.157 **no month to bleed** (Certain alignments of heavenly bodies (studied by astrology) were thought best for medical blood-letting.)

1.1.157 **month** (The 1623 text prints *time* for *month*.)

1.1.158 **let…begun** (compare the proverbial idea expressed in *Romeo and Juliet* 2.5.9: 'These violent delights have violent ends')

1.1.164 **boot** alternative

1.1.165 **Myself** i.e. as opposed to the *gage*

1.1.167 **The…owes** i.e. my duty as a subject puts my life at your disposal

1.1.167 **name** reputation

1.1.168 **that** i.e. *my fair name*

1.1.168 **lives upon my grave** i.e. will be inscribed on my epitaph

1.1.170 **baffled** publicly disgraced (a chivalric term)

1.1.173 **breathed** i.e. uttered

1.1.174 **Lions** (alluding to the lion as king of the beasts and to the lions of the royal coat of arms)

1.1.174 **make leopards tame** (perhaps refers to the heraldic 'lion leopard' (i.e. not rampant, standing) of the Norfolk crest)

1.1.175 **but…spots** (proverbial; from Jeremiah 13:23)

1.1.175 **spots** (quibbling on the spots or 'stains' on reputation)

1.1.177 **mortal times** earthly life

Is spotless reputation; that away,
Men are but gilded loam, or painted clay.
A jewel in a ten-times barred-up chest   180
Is a bold spirit in a loyal breast.
Mine honour is my life; both grow in one.
Take honour from me, and my life is done.
Then, dear my liege, mine honour let me try,
In that I live, and for that will I die.   185

KING RICHARD [*to Bolingbroke*]   Cousin, throw up your gage.
    Do you begin.

BOLINGBROKE   O God defend my soul from such deep sin!
    Shall I seem crest-fallen in my father's sight?
    Or with pale beggar-fear impeach my height,
    Before this out-dared dastard? Ere my tongue   190
    Shall wound my honour with such feeble wrong,
    Or sound so base a parle, my teeth shall tear
    The slavish motive of recanting fear,
    And spit it bleeding in his high disgrace
    Where shame doth harbour, even in Mowbray's face.   195
                                   [*Exit John of Gaunt*]

KING RICHARD   We were not born to sue, but to command,
    Which since we cannot do to make you friends,
    Be ready, as your lives shall answer it,
    At Coventry upon Saint Lambert's Day.
    There shall your swords and lances arbitrate   200
    The swelling difference of your settled hate.
    Since we cannot atone you, we shall see

1.1.179 **Men...clay** (compare the
biblical *whited sepulchres*; Matthew 23:27)
1.1.180–1 **A...breast** i.e. a bold spirit...is
a jewel...
1.1.182 **in one** united
1.1.184 **try** put to the test
1.1.186 **throw up** (The alternative
reading in the 1623 text is *throw down*,
which suggests throwing (or simply
surrendering) the gage to Richard, who
may be seated on a throne. Richard may
be actually be on the upper level of the
stage here. It is possible that the variants
reflect changes in staging.)

1.1.188 **crest-fallen** humbled
1.1.189 **impeach my height** disgrace my
high birth
1.1.191 **such feeble wrong** the injury of
such feebleness
1.1.192 **sound...parle** (metaphor of
a trumpet-call for truce)
1.1.193 **motive** instigator, instrument,
organ
1.1.194 **his** its
1.1.199 **Saint Lambert's Day** i.e.
17 September
1.1.202 **atone** reconcile

Justice design the victor's chivalry.
Lord Marshal, command our officers-at-arms
Be ready to direct these home alarms.   [*Exeunt*] 205

1.2

Sc. 2   *Enter John of Gaunt with the Duchess of Gloucester*

GAUNT   Alas, the part I had in Woodstock's blood
     Doth more solicit me than your exclaims
     To stir against the butchers of his life.
     But since correction lieth in those hands
     Which made the fault that we cannot correct,   5
     Put we our quarrel to the will of heaven,
     Who, when they see the hours ripe on earth,
     Will rain hot vengeance on offenders' heads.

DUCHESS OF GLOUCESTER   Finds brotherhood in thee no sharper
          spur?
     Hath love in thy old blood no living fire?   10
     Edward's seven sons, whereof thyself art one,
     Were as seven vials of his sacred blood,
     Or seven fair branches springing from one root.
     Some of those seven are dried by nature's course,
     Some of those branches by the destinies cut;   15
     But Thomas, my dear lord, my life, my Gloucester,
     One vial full of Edward's sacred blood,
     One flourishing branch of his most royal root,
     Is cracked, and all the precious liquor spilt;
     Is hacked down, and his summer leaves all faded   20

1.1.203 **design** indicate
1.1.203 **design...chivalry** i.e. indicate
  the victor through his skill in chivalric
  combat
1.1.205 **home** (as distinct from Irish rebellion)
1.1.205 **alarms** call to arms, disturbances

Sc. 2 1.2.1 **the part...blood** my
  blood-relationship to Woodstock
1.2.1 **Woodstock's** (The 1623 text revises
  to the figure's usual name, reading
  'Gloucester's', and most modern
  productions accept for clarity's sake.)

1.2.2 **exclaims** exclamations
1.2.4 **correction lieth in** punishment
  depends upon
1.2.4 **those hands** i.e. Richard's
1.2.5 **fault** offence
1.2.5 **correct** put right
1.2.6 **quarrel** cause, dispute
1.2.11 **Edward's** i.e. Edward III's
1.2.15 **the destinies** the Fates, thought of as
  three old women who spun, measured out,
  and cut the thread of life (from classical
  myth). Pronounced as two syllables.
1.2.17 **sacred** revered for its royalty

By envy's hand and murder's bloody axe.
Ah, Gaunt, his blood was thine! That bed, that womb,
That mettle, that self mould that fashioned thee
Made him a man; and though thou liv'st and breathest,
Yet art thou slain in him. Thou dost consent   25
In some large measure to thy father's death,
In that thou seest thy wretched brother die,
Who was the model of thy father's life.
Call it not patience, Gaunt, it is despair.
In suffering thus thy brother to be slaughtered,   30
Thou show'st the naked pathway to thy life,
Teaching stern murder how to butcher thee.
That which in mean men we entitle patience
Is pale cold cowardice in noble breasts.
What shall I say? To safeguard thine own life   35
The best way is to venge my Gloucester's death.

GAUNT   God's is the quarrel, for God's substitute,
His deputy anointed in his sight,
Hath caused his death, the which if wrongfully,
Let heaven revenge, for I may never lift   40
An angry arm against his minister.

DUCHESS OF GLOUCESTER   Where then, alas, may I complain
        myself?

GAUNT   To God, the widow's champion and defence.

DUCHESS OF GLOUCESTER   Why then, I will. Farewell old Gaunt.
Thou goest to Coventry, there to behold   45
Our cousin Hereford and fell Mowbray fight.
O, set my husband's wrongs on Hereford's spear,
That it may enter butcher Mowbray's breast!

1.2.21 **envy's** hatred's
1.2.23 **mettle** substance
1.2.23 **self** same
1.2.28 **model** likeness, reproduction
1.2.31 **naked** defenceless
1.2.33 **mean** common, not *noble*
1.2.36 **venge** avenge
1.2.37-8 **God's is...sight** (a common Renaissance view of kingship)

1.2.41 **minister** agent
1.2.42 **complain** lament
1.2.44 **Why then, I will** (The rest of the speech imagines the effects of divine influence upon the combat.)
1.2.46 **fell** ruthless
1.2.47 **set** i.e. may...sit (an imprecation in the subjunctive)

Or if misfortune miss the first career,
Be Mowbray's sins so heavy in his bosom   50
That they may break his foaming courser's back
And throw the rider headlong in the lists,
A caitiff, recreant to my cousin Hereford!
Farewell, old Gaunt. Thy sometimes brother's wife,
With her companion, grief, must end her life.   55

GAUNT   Sister, farewell. I must to Coventry.
As much good stay with thee as go with me.

DUCHESS OF GLOUCESTER   Yet one word more. Grief boundeth
      where it falls,
Not with the empty hollowness, but weight.
I take my leave before I have begun,   60
For sorrow ends not when it seemeth done.
Commend me to thy brother, Edmund York.
Lo, this is all. Nay, yet depart not so!
Though this be all, do not so quickly go:
I shall remember more. Bid him—ah what?—   65
With all good speed at Pleshey visit me.
Alack, and what shall good old York there see,
But empty lodgings and unfurnished walls,
Unpeopled offices, untrodden stones,
And what hear there for welcome but my groans?   70
Therefore commend me; let him not come there
To seek out sorrow that dwells everywhere.
Desolate, desolate will I hence and die.
The last leave of thee takes my weeping eye.   *Exeunt [severally].*

I.2.49 **misfortune** i.e. to Mowbray
I.2.49 **miss** fails at
I.2.49 **career** charge, encounter
I.2.53 **caitiff** wretched coward (often thought to be an adjective qualifying *recreant* as a noun)
I.2.53 **recreant** surrendering (hence *to*; but other senses are 'apostate' (noun) and 'cowardly')
I.2.54 **sometimes** former
I.2.58 **boundeth** rebounds
I.2.59 **empty hollowness** (as of a ball; also suggesting superficiality)
I.2.66 **Pleshey** (a residence in Essex belonging to the Gloucester family)
I.2.68 **lodgings** rooms
I.2.68 **unfurnished** (perhaps specifically 'without tapestries')
I.2.69 **offices** servants' rooms, or more abstractly their (now vacant) jobs
I.2.72 **everywhere** i.e. in all parts of the house
I.2.73 **Desolate, desolate** (the first pronounced as three syllables, the second as two: 'des'late')

1.3

Sc. 3   *Enter Lord Marshal [with officers] and the Duke Aumerle.*

LORD MARSHAL   My Lord Aumerle, is Harry Hereford armed?

AUMERLE   Yea, at all points, and longs to enter in.

LORD MARSHAL   The Duke of Norfolk, sprightfully and bold,
Stays but the summons of the appellant's trumpet.

AUMERLE   Why then, the champions are prepared, and stay   5
For nothing but his majesty's approach.

> *The trumpets sound and the King enters with [John of Gaunt,*
> *Bushy, Bagot, Green and] his nobles. When they are set, enter*
> *Mowbray the Duke of Norfolk, in arms, defendant [with*
> *a herald. The King and nobles take their seats.]*

KING RICHARD   Marshal, demand of yonder champïon
The cause of his arrival here in arms.
Ask him his name, and orderly proceed
To swear him in the justice of his cause.   10

LORD MARSHAL *[to Mowbray]*   In God's name and the King's,
say who thou art,
And why thou com'st thus knightly clad in arms,
Against what man thou com'st and what thy quarrel.
Speak truly on thy knighthood, and thy oath,
As so defend thee heaven and thy valour.   15

MOWBRAY   My name is Thomas Mowbray, Duke of Norfolk,
Who hither come engagèd by my oath—
Which God defend a knight should violate—
Both to defend my loyalty and truth
To God, my king, and my succeeding issue,   20
Against the Duke of Hereford that appeals me;
And by the grace of God, and this mine arm,
To prove him, in defending of myself,

Sc. 3 1.3.3 **sprightfully** spiritedly   1.3.11 **say who thou art** (This may be
1.3.4 **Stays but** only awaits   asked because the visor of Mowbray's
1.3.4 **appellant's** accuser's   helmet is down.)
1.3.7 **demand of** ask   1.3.13 **quarrel** cause, dispute
1.3.7 **champïon** warrior   1.3.15 **As** to which extent
1.3.9 **orderly** according to the rules   1.3.18 **defend** forbid
1.3.10 **swear him in** make him swear as to

A traitor to my God, my king, and me,
And as I truly fight, defend me heaven!   25

[*Tucket*]. *Enter Bolingbroke Duke of Hereford appellant in*
armour [*and herald*]

KING RICHARD   Marshal, ask yonder knight in arms
Both who he is, and why he cometh hither
Thus plated in habiliments of war;
And formally according to our law
Depose him in the justice of his cause.   30

LORD MARSHAL [*to Bolingbroke*]   What is thy name? And wherefore
        com'st thou hither
Before King Richard in his royal lists?
Against whom com'st thou? And what's thy quarrel?
Speak like a true knight, so defend thee heaven.

BOLINGBROKE   Harry of Hereford, Lancaster and Derby   35
Am I, who ready here do stand in arms
To prove by God's grace, and my body's valour
In lists on Thomas Mowbray, Duke of Norfolk,
That he is a traitor foul and dangerous
To God of heaven, King Richard, and to me;   40
And as I truly fight, defend me heaven!

[*Bolingbroke sits*]

LORD MARSHAL   On pain of death, no person be so bold
Or daring-hardy as to touch the lists
Except the Marshal and such officers
Appointed to direct these fair designs.   45

[*Bolingbroke rises*]

BOLINGBROKE   Lord Marshal, let me kiss my sovereign's hand
And bow my knee before his majesty,
For Mowbray and myself are like two men,
That vow a long and weary pilgrimage;
Then let us take a ceremonious leave   50
And loving farewell of our several friends.

1.3.28 **plated…war** wearing plated battle
    armour
1.3.30 **Depose** examine on oath

1.3.45 **direct…designs** carry out the
    plans fairly
1.3.51 **several** respective

LORD MARSHAL   The appellant in all duty greets your highness,
And craves to kiss your hand and take his leave.

KING RICHARD   We will descend and fold him in our arms.

[*King Richard embraces Bolingbroke*]

Cousin of Hereford, as thy cause is right,   55
So be thy fortune in this royal fight.
Farewell my blood, which if today thou shed
Lament we may, but not revenge thee dead.

BOLINGBROKE   O, let no noble eye profane a tear
For me if I be gored with Mowbray's spear.   60
As confident as is the falcon's flight
Against a bird do I with Mowbray fight.
[*To the Lord Marshal*] My loving lord, I take my leave of you:
[*To Aumerle*] Of you, my noble cousin, Lord Aumerle;
Not sick, although I have to do with death,   65
But lusty, young, and cheerly drawing breath.
Lo, as at English feasts so I regreet
The daintiest last, to make the end most sweet.
[*To Gaunt*] O thou, the earthly author of my blood,
Whose youthful spirit in me regenerate   70
Doth with a two-fold vigour lift me up
To reach at victory above my head,
Add proof unto mine armour with thy prayers,
And with thy blessings steel my lance's point,
That it may enter Mowbray's waxen coat   75

1.3.55 **as** in so far as
1.3.58 **not...dead** Bolingbroke's defeat would be taken to show him guilty of treachery.
1.3.59 **profane** misuse
1.3.66 **cheerly** in good cheer
1.3.67 **regreet** greet
1.3.69 **earthly** i.e. as distinct from God
1.3.69 **author** originator, begetter
1.3.70 **spirit** (here, as often, one syllable)
1.3.70 **regenerate** formed afresh, reborn
1.3.71 **two-fold vigour** i.e. with his own vigour and that of his father
1.3.73 **proof** invulnerability
1.3.74 **steel** harden
1.3.75 **waxen coat** armour as penetrable as wax

And furbish new the name of John o' Gaunt,
Even in the lusty haviour of his son.

GAUNT   God in thy good cause make thee prosperous.
Be swift like lightning in the execution,
And let thy blows, doubly redoubëlèd,   80
Fall like amazing thunder on the casque
Of thy adverse pernicious enemy.
Rouse up thy youthful blood, be valiant, and live.

BOLINGBROKE   Mine innocence and Saint George to thrive!

MOWBRAY   However God or fortune cast my lot,   85
There lives or dies, true to King Richard's throne,
A loyal, just, and upright gentleman.
Never did captive with a freer heart
Cast off his chains of bondage, and embrace
His golden uncontrolled enfranchisement,   90
More than my dancing soul doth celebrate
This feast of battle with mine adversary.
Most mighty liege, and my companion peers,
Take from my mouth the wish of happy years.
As gentle, and as jocund as to jest,   95
Go I to fight. Truth hath a quiet breast.

KING RICHARD   Farewell, my lord. Securely I espy
Virtue with valour couchèd in thine eye,
Order the trial, Marshal, and begin.

LORD MARSHAL   Harry of Hereford, Lancaster, and Derby,   100
Receive thy lance, and God defend the right!

[*An officer bears a lance to Bolingbroke*]

BOLINGBROKE   Strong as a tower in hope, I cry, 'Amen!'.

1.3.77 **haviour** behaviour
1.3.81 **amazing** stupefying
1.3.81 **casque** helmet
1.3.83 **valiant** (pronounced as three syllables)
1.3.83–4 **live...thrive** (no rhyme)
1.3.84 **Mine...thrive** (This probably continues from Gaunt's last line: *live...to thrive*.)

1.3.90 **uncontrolled enfranchisement** liberation from bondage
1.3.95 **jest** a sport or entertainment
1.3.96 **Truth...breast** (from proverbial 'Truth fears no trial')
1.3.97 **Securely** confidently (qualifying *couchèd*)
1.3.102 **Strong...hope** (from Psalms 61:3)

LORD MARSHAL [*to an officer*]   Go bear this lance to Thomas,
    Duke of Norfolk.

   [*An officer bears a lance to Mowbray*]

FIRST HERALD   Harry of Hereford, Lancaster, and Derby
    Stands here, for God, his sovereign, and himself,   105
    On pain to be found false and recreant,
    To prove the Duke of Norfolk, Thomas Mowbray,
    A traitor to his God, his king, and him,
    And dares him to set forward to the fight.

SECOND HERALD   Here standeth Thomas Mowbray, Duke of   110
    Norfolk
    On pain to be found false and recreant,
    Both to defend himself and to approve
    Henry of Hereford, Lancaster, and Derby,
    To God, his sovereign, and to him disloyal,
    Courageously, and with a free desire   115
    Attending but the signal to begin.

LORD MARSHAL   Sound trumpets, and [*to Bolingbroke and
    Mowbray*] set forward, combatants.

   [*A charge is sounded*]

   [*The King throws down his warder*]

Stay, the King hath thrown his warder down.

KING RICHARD   Let them lay by their helmets and their spears,
    And both return back to their chairs again.   120

   [*The combatants disarm and sit down in their chairs*]

[*To the nobles*] Withdraw with us, and let the trumpets sound
While we return these dukes what we decree.

   [*A long flourish*]

[*To Bolingbroke and Mowbray*] Draw near and list what with
our council we have done.

1.3.106 **to be** of being
1.3.109 **dares** challenges
1.3.112 **approve** prove
1.3.117.1 *charge* signal for attack (probably
   sounded on a trumpet)

1.3.117.2 *warder* truncheon, staff (used
   to signal the beginning or end
   of combat)
1.3.122 **While** until
1.3.122 **return** deliver to

For that our kingdom's earth should not be soiled
With that dear blood which it hath fosterèd,   125
And for our eyes do hate the dire aspect
Of civil wounds plowed up with neighbours' swords,
And for we think the eagle-wingèd pride
Of sky-aspiring and ambitious thoughts,
With rival-hating envy, set on you   130
To wake our peace, which in our country's cradle
Draws the sweet infant breath of gentle sleep,
Which so roused up with boist'rous untuned drums,
With harsh-resounding trumpets' dreadful bray
And grating shock of wrathful iron arms,   135
Might from our quiet confines fright fair peace
And make us wade even in our kindred's blood:
Therefore we banish you our territories.
You, cousin Hereford, upon pain of life,
Til twice five summers have enriched our fields   140
Shall not regreet our fair dominïons,
But tread the stranger paths of banishment.

BOLINGBROKE   Your will be done. This must my comfort be:
That sun that warms you here shall shine on me,
And those his golden beams to you here lent   145
Shall point on me, and gild my banishment.

KING RICHARD   Norfolk, for thee remains a heavier doom,
Which I with some unwillingness pronounce:
The sly slow hours shall not determinate
The dateless limit of thy dear exile.   150
The hopeless word of 'never to return'
Breathe I against thee, upon pain of life.

MOWBRAY   A heavy sentence, my most sovereign liege,

1.3.124 **For that** in order that
1.3.126 **for** because
1.3.126 **aspect** spectacle
1.3.128–32 **And...sleep** (This passage was not included in the Folio.)
1.3.128 **for** because
1.3.130 **envy** malice
1.3.130 **set on you** set you on
1.3.139, 152 **life** forfeit of life, death

1.3.141 **regreet** greet again
1.3.142 **stranger** foreign
1.3.144 **That...me** ('The sun shines on all alike' is proverbial.)
1.3.147 **doom** punishment
1.3.149 **sly** stealthy
1.3.149 **determinate** bring to an end
1.3.150 **dateless limit** limitless period
1.3.150 **dear** hard, grievous

And all unlooked-for from your highness' mouth.
A dearer merit, not so deep a maim   155
As to be cast forth in the common air,
Have I deservèd at your highness' hands.
The language I have learnt these forty years,
My native English, now I must forgo,
And now my tongue's use is to me no more   160
Than an unstringèd viol or a harp,
Or like a cunning instrument cased up,
Or, being open, put into his hands
That knows no touch to tune the harmony.
Within my mouth you have engaoled my tongue,   165
Doubly portcullised with my teeth and lips,
And dull unfeeling barren ignorance
Is made my gaoler to attend on me.
I am too old to fawn upon a nurse,
Too far in years to be a pupil now.   170
What is thy sentence then but speechless death,
Which robs my tongue from breathing native breath?

KING RICHARD   It boots thee not to be compassionate.
After our sentence plaining comes too late.

MOWBRAY   Then thus I turn me from my country's light,   175
To dwell in solemn shades of endless night.

KING RICHARD   Return again, and take an oath with thee.

[*To both*] Lay on our royal sword your banished hands.

Swear by the duty that you owe to God—
Our part therein we banish with yourselves—   180

1.3.155 **dearer merit** better reward
1.3.155 **maim** injury
1.3.160 **my tongue's use** my ability to
   speak; the use of my native language
1.3.161 **unstringèd** out of tune
   (alternatively, 'stringless')
1.3.161 **viol** (a stringed instrument)
1.3.162 **cunning** skilfully made; expressive
1.3.163 **open** out of its case
1.3.163 **his** one whose
1.3.164 **knows no touch** has no skill in
   playing

1.3.169 **a nurse** (seen as the person who
   first teaches a child to speak)
1.3.172 **Which** i.e. *thy sentence*
1.3.172 **breathing native breath** speaking
   its native language
1.3.173 **boots** helps
1.3.173 **compassionate** sorrowful or
   piteous
1.3.174 **plaining** lamenting
1.3.180 **Our part therein** i.e. your
   allegiance to me as God's deputy

To keep the oath that we administer:
You never shall, so help you truth and God,
Embrace each other's love in banishment,
Nor never look upon each other's face,
Nor never write, regreet, nor reconcile   185
This low'ring tempest of your home-bred hate,
Nor never by advisèd purpose meet
To plot, contrive, or complot any ill
'Gainst us, our state, our subjects, or our land.

BOLINGBROKE   I swear.   190

MOWBRAY   And I, to keep all this.

BOLINGBROKE   Norfolk, so far as to mine enemy:
By this time, had the King permitted us,
One of our souls had wandered in the air,
Banished this frail sepùlchre of our flesh,
As now our flesh is banished from this land.   195
Confess thy treasons ere thou fly the realm.
Since thou hast far to go, bear not along
The clogging burden of a guilty soul.

MOWBRAY   No, Bolingbroke, if ever I were traitor
My name be blotted from the book of life,   200
And I from heaven banished as from hence.
But what thou art, God, thou, and I, do know,
And all too soon, I fear, the King shall rue.

[*To King Richard*] Farewell, my liege. Now no way can I stray.

Save back to England, all the world's my way.   *Exit* 205

KING RICHARD [*to Gaunt*]   Uncle, even in the glasses of thine eyes
I see thy grievèd heart. Thy sad aspect
Hath from the number of his banished years

1.3.187 **advisèd** deliberate
1.3.191 **so far as to** i.e. (I speak) to the extent befitting
1.3.198 **clogging** encumbering
1.3.200 **My...life** (from Revelation 3:5)
1.3.200 **life** i.e. eternal life

1.3.204 **stray** i.e. lose my way
1.3.206 **glasses** windows
1.3.207 **aspect** appearance (accented on the second syllable)
1.3.208 **banished years** years of banishment

Plucked four away. *[To Bolingbroke]* Six frozen winters spent,
Return with welcome home from banishment.   210

BOLINGBROKE   How long a time lies in one little word!
Four lagging winters and four wanton springs
End in a word, such is the breath of kings.

GAUNT   I thank my liege that in regard of me
He shortens four years of my son's exile;   215
But little vantage shall I reap thereby,
For ere the six years that he hath to spend
Can change their moons and bring their times about,
My oil-dried lamp and time-bewasted light
Shall be extinct with age and endless night,   220
My inch of taper will be burnt and done,
And blindfold death not let me see my son.

KING RICHARD   Why, uncle, thou hast many years to live.

GAUNT   But not a minute, King, that thou canst give.
Shorten my days thou canst with sullen sorrow,   225
And pluck nights from me, but not lend a morrow.
Thou canst help time to furrow me with age,
But stop no wrinkle in his pilgrimage.
Thy word is current with him for my death,
But dead, thy kingdom cannot buy my breath.   230

KING RICHARD   Thy son is banished upon good advice,
Whereto thy tongue a party verdict gave.
Why at our justice seem'st thou then to lour?

GAUNT   Things sweet to taste prove in digestion sour.
You urged me as a judge, but I had rather   235

1.3.212 **wanton** luxuriant
1.3.215 **exile** (accented on the second syllable)
1.3.217 **spend** waste, lose
1.3.218 **times** seasons
1.3.218 **about** around
1.3.219 **time-bewasted** consumed by time
1.3.220 **extinct with** extinguished by
1.3.222 **blindfold** because the dead are sightless; death's emblem is an eyeless skull; death is seen as a hooded figure; or death is itself the blindfold

1.3.225 **sorrow** a cause of grief
1.3.228 **pilgrimage** journey, progress (developed from the idea of life's pilgrimage)
1.3.229 **current** valid (like a coin *current* by royal authority)
1.3.230 **dead** when I am dead
1.3.232 **party verdict** share in the joint verdict
1.3.234 **Things...sour** (proverbial; from Revelation 10:9–10)

You would have bid me argue like a father.
O, had it been a stranger, not my child,
To smooth his fault I should have been more mild.
A partial slander sought I to avoid,
And in the sentence my own life destroyed.   240
Alas, I looked when some of you should say
I was too strict to make mine own away,
But you gave leave to my unwilling tongue
Against my will to do myself this wrong.

KING RICHARD   Cousin, farewell; and, uncle, bid him so.   245
Six years we banish him and he shall go.

[*Flourish. Exeunt all but Aumerle, the Lord Marshal, John of
Gaunt, and Bolingbroke*]

AUMERLE [*to Bolingbroke*]   Cousin, farewell. What presence must
    not know,
From where you do remain let paper show.   [*Exit*]

LORD MARSHAL [*to Bolingbroke*]   My lord, no leave take I,
    for I will ride
As far as land will let me by your side.   250

GAUNT [*to Bolingbroke*]   O, to what purpose dost thou hoard thy
    words,
That thou return'st no greeting to thy friends?

BOLINGBROKE   I have too few to take my leave of you,
When the tongue's office should be prodigal
To breathe the abundant dolour of the heart.   255

GAUNT [*to Bolingbroke*]   Thy grief is but thy absence for a time.

BOLINGBROKE   Joy absent, grief is present for that time.

GAUNT   What is six winters? They are quickly gone.

BOLINGBROKE   To men in joy, but grief makes one hour ten.

1.3.237–40 **O...destroyed** (This passage
was not included in the Folio.)
1.3.238 **To smooth** in order to gloss over
1.3.239 **partial slander** false accusation of
partiality
1.3.241 **looked when** expected that
1.3.242 **to...away** in disposing of my own
(son)

1.3.247 **What...know** what you cannot
tell me personally because of your
absence
1.3.248 **remain** stay
1.3.254 **office** functions
1.3.255 **To breathe** in breathing
1.3.256 **grief** grievance; sorrow (but
specifically 'sorrow' in 1.3.248)

GAUNT   Call it a travel that thou tak'st for pleasure.   260

BOLINGBROKE   My heart will sigh when I miscall it so,
Which finds it an enforcèd pilgrimage.

GAUNT   The sullen passage of thy weary steps,
Esteem as foil wherein thou art to set
The precious jewel of thy home return.   265

BOLINGBROKE   Nay, rather, every tedious stride I make
Will but remember what a deal of world
I wander from the jewels that I love.
Must I not serve a long apprenticehood
To foreign passages, and in the end,   270
Having my freedom, boast of nothing else
But that I was a journeyman to grief?

GAUNT   All places that the eye of heaven visits
Are to a wise man ports and happy havens.
Teach thy necessity to reason thus: 275
There is no virtue like necessity.
Think not the King did banish thee,
But thou the King. Woe doth the heavier sit
Where it perceives it is but faintly borne.
Go, say I sent thee forth to purchase honour,   280
And not the King exiled thee; or suppose
Devouring pestilence hangs in our air
And thou art flying to a fresher clime.
Look what thy soul holds dear, imagine it
To lie that way thou goest, not whence thou com'st.   285
Suppose the singing birds musicians,
The grass whereon thou tread'st, the presence strewed,

1.3.264 **foil** the setting of a *jewel*
1.3.267 **remember** remind
1.3.267 **deal** extent
1.3.270 **To** i.e. indentured in
1.3.271 **freedom** qualification as
a *journeyman*; repeal from banishment
1.3.272 **was** i.e. must be (The narrative of
the image confusingly allows it to slip
into the past tense.)
1.3.272 **journeyman** qualified artisan
(freed from the apprenticeship of exile to
find himself a wage-slave to *grief*; with a

quibble in the *journey* of exile suggesting,
perhaps, alienation from joy)
1.3.273–4 **All…havens** (proverbial)
1.3.273 **eye of heaven** sun
1.3.276 **There…necessity** (from
the proverb 'to make a virtue of
necessity')
1.3.279 **faintly** faint-heartedly
1.3.280 **purchase** acquire
1.3.284 **Look what** whatever
1.3.287 **presence strewed** royal presence-
chamber, strewed with rushes

The flowers, fair ladies, and thy steps no more
Than a delightful measure or a dance;
For gnarling sorrow hath less power to bite   290
The man that mocks at it and sets it light.

BOLINGBROKE   O, who can hold a fire in his hand
By thinking on the frosty Caucasus?
Or cloy the hungry edge of appetite,
By bare imagination of a feast?   295
Or wallow naked in December snow,
By thinking on fantastic summer's heat?
O no, the apprehension of the good,
Gives but the greater feeling to the worse.
Fell sorrow's tooth doth never rankle more   300
Than when he bites but lanceth not the sore.

GAUNT   Come, come, my son, I'll bring thee on thy way.
Had I thy youth and cause, I would not stay.

BOLINGBROKE   Then England's ground farewell, sweet soil, adieu,
My mother and my nurse that bears me yet!   305
Where'er I wander, boast of this I can:
Though banished, yet a true-born Englishman.   *Exeunt.*

1.4

Sc. 4   *Enter the King with [Green and Bagot] at one door, and
the Lord Aumerle at another*

KING RICHARD   We did observe. Cousin Aumerle,
How far brought you high Hereford on his way?

AUMERLE   I brought high Hereford, if you call him so,
But to the next highway, and there I left him.

KING RICHARD   And say, what store of parting tears were shed?   5

AUMERLE   Faith, none for me, except the northeast wind,

1.3.289 **measure** (a stately dance)
1.3.290 **gnarling** snarling
1.3.291 **sets it light** values it
    lightly
1.3.297 **fantastic** imagined
1.3.300 **Fell** fierce
1.3.302 **bring** escort

1.3.303 **stay** linger in England; or stay in exile
    (If the latter, the line is probably an aside.)
Sc. 4 1.4.1 **We did observe** (replying to
    a remark from Bagot and Greene)
1.4.4 **highway** (quibbling on Richard's
    words)
1.4.6 **for me** for my part

Which then blew bitterly against our faces,
Awaked the sleeping rheum, and so by chance
Did grace our hollow parting with a tear.

KING RICHARD   What said our cousin when you parted with him?   10

AUMERLE   'Farewell'. And for my heart disdainèd that my tongue
Should so profane the word, that taught me craft
To counterfeit oppression of such grief
That words seemed buried in my sorrow's grave.
Marry, would the word 'farewell' have lengthened hours   15
And added years to his short banishment,
He should have had a volume of farewells;
But since it would not, he had none of me.

KING RICHARD   He is our cousin, cousin; but 'tis doubt,
When time shall call him home from banishment,   20
Whether our kinsman come to see his friends.
Ourself and Bushy, Bagot here, and Green
Observed his courtship to the common people,
How he did seem to dive into their hearts
With humble and familiar courtesy,   25
What reverence he did throw away on slaves,
Wooing poor craftsmen with the craft of smiles
And patient underbearing of his fortune,
As 'twere to banish their affects with him.
Off goes his bonnet to an oysterwench,   30
A brace of draymen bid God speed him well,
And had the tribute of his supple knee
With, 'Thanks, my countrymen, my loving friends',
As were our England in reversion his,

1.4.8 **rheum** tears
1.4.9 **hollow** insincere
1.4.11 **for** because
1.4.12 **profane** abuse
1.4.12 **that** i.e. his heart's disdain
1.4.12 **craft** skill
1.4.13 **oppression** distress
1.4.15 **Marry** indeed
1.4.19 **our cousin, cousin** (Richard, Bolingbroke, and Aumerle were sons of three brothers.)
1.4.21 **come…friends** i.e. will be allowed to visit his kinsmen

1.4.25 **familiar** affable
1.4.28 **underbearing** enduring
1.4.29 **As 'twere** i.e. as if attempting
1.4.29 **affects** affections
1.4.30 **bonnet** cap
1.4.32 **his supple knee** i.e. a willingly given low bow
1.4.34 **in reversion** (a legal term for a property due to revert to the original owner on the death of the lessee or expiring of the contract)

And he our subjects' next degree in hope.   35

GREEN   Well, he is gone, and with him go these thoughts.
Now for the rebels which stand out in Ireland.
Expedient manage must be made, my liege,
Ere further leisure yield them further means
For their advantage and your highness' loss.   40

KING RICHARD   We will ourself in person to this war,
And for, our coffers with too great a court
And liberal largess are grown somewhat light,
We are enforced to farm our royal realm,
The revenue whereof shall furnish us   45
For our affairs in hand. If that come short,
Our substitutes, at home shall have blank charters,
Whereto, when they shall know what men are rich,
They shall subscribe them, for large sums of gold,
And send them after to supply our wants;   50
For we will make for Ireland presently.

   Enter Bushy

Bushy, what news?

BUSHY   Old John of Gaunt is grievous sick, my lord,
Suddenly taken, and hath sent post-haste,
To entreat your majesty to visit him.   55

KING RICHARD   Where lies he?

BUSHY   At Ely House.

KING RICHARD   Now put it, God, in the physician's mind
To help him to his grave immediately!
The lining of his coffers shall make coats   60
To deck our soldiers for these Irish wars.
Come, gentlemen, let's all go visit him.
Pray God we may make haste and come too late!

[ALL]   Amen.   *Exeunt.*

1.4.38 **Expedient manage** hasty arrangements
1.4.42 **for** because
1.4.44 **farm our royal realm** i.e. lease out the king's feudal rights to gather taxes
1.4.47 **substitutes** deputies
1.4.47 **blank charters** (documents which the *substitutes* could fill in as they pleased, enabling them to raise the required money in forced loans from the rich)
1.4.49 **subscribe them** fill them (the charter) in, or put them (the rich men) down
1.4.60 **lining** contents (quibbling on 'lining cloth')

Sc. 5   *Enter John of Gaunt sick, [carried in a chair by attendants,]*
       with the Duke of York]

GAUNT   Will the King come, that I may breathe my last
  In wholesome counsel to his unstaid youth?

YORK   Vex not yourself, nor strive not with your breath,
  For all in vain comes counsel to his ear.

GAUNT   O, but they say the tongues of dying men   5
  Enforce attention like deep harmony.
  Where words are scarce they are seldom spent in vain,
  For they breathe truth that breathe their words in pain.
  He that no more must say is listened more
    Than they whom youth and ease have taught to glose.   10
  More are men's ends marked than their lives before.
    The setting sun, and music at the close,
  As the last taste of sweets, is sweetest last,
  Writ in remembrance more than things long past.
  Though Richard my life's counsel would not hear,   15
  My death's sad tale may yet undeaf his ear.

YORK   No, it is stopped with other, flattering sounds,
  As praises of whose taste the wise are feared,
  Lascivious metres to whose venom sound
  The open ear of youth doth always listen,   20
  Report of fashions in proud Italy,
  Whose manners still our tardy-apish nation
  Limps after in base imitation.
  Where doth the world thrust forth a vanity—
  So it be new, there's no respect how vile—   25
  That is not quickly buzzed into his ears?
  Then all too late comes counsel to be heard,
  Where will doth mutiny with wit's regard.

Sc. 5 2.1.2 **unstaid** unruly
2.1.3 **breath** i.e. speech
2.1.5–6 **the…harmony** (proverbial)
2.1.9 **listened** listened to
2.1.10 **glose** talk speciously
2.1.12 **close** cadence, conclusion
2.1.18 **feared** apprehensive, wary

2.1.19 **venom** venomous
2.1.22 **tardy-apish** imitative but out of date
2.1.25 **So** if
2.1.25 **respect** regard for
2.1.28 **with** against
2.1.28 **wit's regard** paying heed to sound
  judgement

Direct not him whose way himself will choose.
'Tis breath thou lack'st, and that breath wilt thou lose. 30
GAUNT   Methinks I am a prophet new inspired,
And thus expiring do foretell of him.
His rash, fierce blaze of riot cannot last,
For violent fires soon burn out themselves;
Small showers last long, but sudden storms are short. 35
He tires betimes that spurs too fast betimes.
With eager feeding food doth choke the feeder.
Light vanity, insatiate cormorant,
Consuming means, soon prays upon itself.
This royal throne of kings, this sceptred isle, 40
This earth of majesty, this seat of Mars,
This other Eden, demi-paradise,
This fortress built by nature for herself
Against infection and the hand of war,
This happy breed of men, this little world, 45
This precious stone set in the silver sea,
Which serves it in the office of a wall,
Or as a moat defensive to a house
Against the envy of less happier lands;
This blessèd plot, this earth, this realm, this England, 50
This nurse, this teeming womb of royal kings,
Feared by their breed, and famous by their birth,
Renownèd for their deeds as far from home
For Christian service and true chivalry
As is the sepulchre in stubborn Jewry, 55
Of the world's ransom, blessèd Mary's son;

2.1.31–2 **inspired…expiring** (grim wordplay on *breath*, 2.1.30)
2.1.33–9 **His…itself** (images varying the proverbial 'Nothing violent can be permanent')
2.1.33 **rash** (with a probable secondary sense, 'quick and strong')
2.1.36 **betimes** soon, early
2.1.38 **cormorant** rapacious glutton (as the bird supposedly is)
2.1.39 **Consuming means** having consumed available resources
2.1.41 **earth** land
2.1.41 **seat** dwelling-place
2.1.42 **demi** (possibly 'little', 'half', or 'one of two')
2.1.45 **happy breed** fortunate race
2.1.47 **office** function
2.1.49 **envy** malice
2.1.52–6 **Feared…son** (alluding to the deeds of English kings in the Crusades)
2.1.52 **Feared by** feared on account of
2.1.55 **stubborn Jewry** (the land of the Jews, resistant to Christianity)

This land of such dear souls, this dear, dear land,
Dear for her reputation through the world,
Is now leased out—I die pronouncing it—
Like to a tenement or pelting farm.   60
England, bound in with the triumphant sea,
Whose rocky shore beats back the envious siege
Of wat'ry Neptune, is now bound in with shame,
With inky blots and rotten parchment bonds.
That England that was wont to conquer others   65
Hath made a shameful conquest of itself.
Ah, would the scandal vanish with my life,
How happy then were my ensuing death!

    [*Flourish*]

YORK   The King is come. Deal mildly with his youth,
For young hot colts, being reined, do rage the more.   70

    Enter King, Queen; [the Duke of Aumerle, Bushy, Green,
    Bagot, Ross, and Willoughby]

QUEEN   How fares our noble uncle Lancaster?

KING RICHARD   What comfort, man? How is't with agèd Gaunt?

GAUNT   O, how that name befits my composition!
Old Gaunt indeed, and gaunt in being old.
Within me grief hath kept a tedious fast,   75
And who abstains from meat that is not gaunt?
For sleeping England long time have I watched.
Watching breeds leanness, leanness is all gaunt.
The pleasure that some fathers feed upon
Is my strict fast; I mean my children's looks;   80
And therein fasting hast thou made me gaunt.
Gaunt am I for the grave, gaunt as a grave
Whose hollow womb inherits naught but bones.

KING RICHARD   Can sick men play so nicely with their names?

2.1.60 **tenement** tenanted property
2.1.60 **pelting** worthless
2.1.61 **with** by
2.1.62 **envious** (in the modern sense)
2.1.64 **rotten** corrupt
2.1.67 **scandal** disgrace
2.1.73 **composition** constitution

2.1.75 **tedious** laborious, painful
2.1.78 **Watching** sleeplessness
2.1.80 **my children's looks** (referring to Bolingbroke's exile)
2.1.81 **therein fasting** making me fast in that way
2.1.84 **nicely** subtly, equivocally

GAUNT   No, misery makes sport to mock itself.   85
    Since thou dost seek to kill my name in me,
    I mock my name, great King, to flatter thee.

KING RICHARD   Should dying men flatter with those that live?

GAUNT   No, no, men living flatter those that die.

KING RICHARD   Thou now a-dying sayest thou flatterest me.   90

GAUNT   O no: thou diest, though I the sicker be.

KING RICHARD   I am in health; I breathe, and see thee ill.

GAUNT   Now He that made me knows I see thee ill:
    Ill in myself to see, and in thee seeing ill.
    Thy deathbed is no lesser than thy land,   95
    Wherein thou liest in reputation sick;
    And thou, too careless-patient as thou art,
    Committ'st thy anointed body to the cure
    Of those physicians that first wounded thee.
    A thousand flatterers sit within thy crown,   100
    Whose compass is no bigger than thy head,
    And yet encagèd in so small a verge
    The waste is no whit lesser than thy land.
    O, had thy grandsire with a prophet's eye
    Seen how his son's son should destroy his sons,   105
    From forth thy reach he would have laid thy shame,
    Deposing thee before thou wert possessed,
    Which art possessed now to depose thyself.
    Why, cousin, wert thou regent of the world
    It were a shame to let this land by lease.   110

2.1.85 **misery** (as opposed to sickness)

2.1.85 **makes…itself** finds amusement in mocking itself

2.1.86 **kill my name** destroy my family reputation (by the exile of Bolingbroke)

2.1.94 **Ill…ill** i.e. too ill to see well myself, and seeing evil in you

2.1.98 **anointed** (quibbling on the ritual anointing of a king and medicinal anointment)

2.1.101 **compass** circle, area

2.1.102 **verge** circle of metal; area of 12 miles around the court controlled by the king's marshal; a measure of an area of land (15–30 acres)

2.1.103 **waste** destruction (specifically injury done to a property by its tenant); useless expense; *waist*, narrowed port

2.1.105 **his son** i.e. Gloucester and Gaunt himself (*thy grandsire* Edward III's sons)

2.1.106 **From forth** out of

2.1.107 **possessed** in possession of the crown (but in 2.1.108, 'friendly determined')

2.1.108 **Which** who

2.1.109 **cousin** kinsman

2.1.109 **regent** ruler

But for thy world enjoying but this land,
Is it not more than shame to shame it so?
Landlord of England art thou now, not King.
Thy state of law is bondslave to the law,
And thou—   115

KING RICHARD   —A lunatic lean-witted fool,
Presuming on an ague's privilege!
Dar'st with thy frozen admonition
Make pale our cheek, chasing the royal blood
With fury from his native residence.   120
Now by my seat's right royal majesty,
Wert thou not brother to great Edward's son,
This tongue that runs so roundly in thy head
Should run thy head from thy unreverent shoulders.

GAUNT   O, spare me not, my brother Edward's son,   125
For that I was his father Edward's son.
That blood already, like the pelican,
Hast thou tapped out and drunkenly caroused.
My brother Gloucester, plain well-meaning soul,
Whom fair befall in heaven 'mongst happy souls,   130
May be a precedent and witness good
That thou respect'st not spilling Edward's blood.
Join with the present sickness that I have,
And thy unkindness be like crooked age,
To crop at once a too-long-withered flower.   135
Live in thy shame, but die not shame with thee.

2.1.114 **state of law** legal status
2.1.115–16 **And thou…A** (In the 1623 text,
   Richard interrupts Gaunt and begins his
   line with 'And thou a', matching Gaunt's
   curse and interrupting Gaunt before
   Gaunt can get the word out. In the 1597
   version, printed here, the King's temper
   may erupt more suddenly.)
2.1.117 **ague's privilege** i.e. the privilege
   of the sick
2.1.118 **frozen** unfeeling, deathly cold
2.1.118 **admonition** (pronounced as five
   syllables)
2.1.120 **his native residence** i.e. the liver,
   thought of as being the seat of the passions

2.1.120 **native** natural
2.1.123 **roundly** bluntly; or glibly
2.1.125 **my brother Edward** (Edward the
   Black Prince, son of Edward III, and
   Richard's father)
2.1.127 **pelican** (A mother pelican
   supposedly wounded herself to supply
   blood which would feed her young. This
   was taken as an emblem of self-sacrifice
   or, in the case of the young bird, of filial
   ingratitude.)
2.1.130 **fair befall** may happiness await
2.1.131 **precedent** sign, indication
2.1.132 **thou respect'st not** you don't care
   about

These words hereafter thy tormentors be.

[*To attendants*] Convey me to my bed, then to my grave.

Love they to live that love and honour have.

                                        Exit [*carried in the chair*].

KING RICHARD   And let them die that age and sullens have;   140
For both hast thou, and both become the grave.

YORK   I do beseech your majesty, impute his words
To wayward sickliness and age in him.
He loves you, on my life, and holds you dear
As Harry Duke of Hereford, were he here.   145

KING RICHARD   Right, you say true: as Hereford's love, so his;
As theirs, so mine; and all be as it is.

    [*Enter the Earl of Northumberland*]

NORTHUMBERLAND   My liege, old Gaunt commends him to your
        majesty.

KING RICHARD   What says he?

NORTHUMBERLAND   Nay, nothing, all is said.
His tongue is now a stringless instrument.   150
Words, life, and all, old Lancaster hath spent.

YORK   Be York the next that must be bankrupt so!
Though death be poor, it ends a mortal woe.

KING RICHARD   The ripest fruit first falls, and so doth he.
His time is spent; our pilgrimage must be.   155
So much for that. Now for our Irish wars.
We must supplant those rough rug-headed kerns,
Which live like venom where no venom else
But only they have privilege to live;
And for these great affairs do ask some charge.   160

2.1.136 **die...thee** may shame outlive you;
or may shame always live with you

2.1.140 **sullens** sulks

2.1.145 **As...Hereford** i.e. as Gaunt
loves his son; Richard deliberately
misinterprets 'as Hereford loves
Richard'

2.1.148 **him** himself

2.1.154 **The...falls** (proverbial)

2.1.155 **be** i.e. continue

2.1.157 **rug-headed** shaggy-headed

2.1.157 **kerns** notoriously wild Irish
foot-soldiers

2.1.158-9 **where...live** (alluding to the
legend that St Patrick drove all snakes
out of Ireland)

2.1.160 **ask some charge** demand some
expenditure

Towards our assistance we do seize to us
The plate, coin, revenues, and movables
Whereof our uncle Gaunt did stand possessed.

YORK   How long shall I be patient? Ah, how long
Shall tender duty make me suffer wrong?   165
Not Gloucester's death, nor Hereford's banishment,
Nor Gaunt's rebukes, nor England's private wrongs,
Nor the prevention of poor Bolingbroke
About his marriage, nor my own disgrace,
Have ever made me sour my patient cheek,   170
Or bend one wrinkle on my sovereign's face.
I am the last of noble Edward's sons,
Of whom thy father, Prince of Wales, was first.
In war was never lion raged more fierce,
In peace was never gentle lamb more mild,   175
Than was that young and princely gentleman.
His face thou hast, for even so looked he,
Accomplished with the number of thy hours.
But when he frowned it was against the French,
And not against his friends. His noble hand   180
Did win what he did spend, and spent not that
Which his triumphant father's hand had won.
His hands were guilty of no kindred blood,
But bloody with the enemies of his kin.
O Richard, York is too far gone with grief,   185
Or else he never would compare between.

KING RICHARD   Why, uncle, what's the matter?

YORK   O my liege,
Pardon me if you please; if not, I, pleased
Not to be pardoned, am content withal.

2.1.161 **Towards** (pronounced as one syllable)
2.1.162 **plate** gold and silver utensils
2.1.165 **tender** scrupulous
2.1.167 **private wrongs** wrongs committed against private individuals
2.1.168–9 **the…marriage** (an isolated allusion to Richard's intervention against Bolingbroke's proposed marriage in exile to the King of France's cousin)
2.1.171 **bend one wrinkle** i.e. frown
2.1.174 **lion raged more fierce** enraged lion more fierce; or lion who raged more fiercely
2.1.178 **Accomplished…hours** i.e. when he was your age
2.1.178 **Accomplished** furnished

Seek you to seize and grip into your hands 190
The royalties and rights of banished Hereford?
Is not Gaunt dead? And doth not Hereford live?
Was not Gaunt just? And is not Harry true?
Did not the one deserve to have an heir?
Is not his heir a well-deserving son? 195
Take Hereford's rights away, and take from Time
His charters and his customary rights:
Let not tomorrow then ensue today;
Be not thyself, for how art thou a king
But by fair sequence and succession? 200
Now afore God—God forbid I say true—
If you do wrongfully seize Hereford's rights,
Call in the letters patents that he hath
By his attorneys-general to sue
His livery, and deny his offered homage, 205
You pluck a thousand dangers on your head,
You lose a thousand well-disposèd hearts,
And prick my tender patience to those thoughts
Which honour and allegiance cannot think.

KING RICHARD   Think what you will, we seize into our hands 210
His plate, his goods, his money, and his lands.

YORK   I'll not be by the while. My liege, farewell.
What will ensue hereof there's none can tell;
But by bad courses may be understood
That their events can never fall out good.   *Exit* 215

KING RICHARD   Go, Bushy, to the Earl of Wiltshire straight,

2.1.190 **grip** seize, clutch
2.1.191 **royalties** rights granted by a king
2.1.193 **true** legal
2.1.198 **ensue** follow upon
2.1.199 **Be not thyself** (suggesting that Richard's 'self' of kingship will be annihilated as a consequence of his disinheriting Bolingbroke)
2.1.203 **Call in** revoke
2.1.203 **letters patents** (documents issued by Richard allowing Bolingbroke to make a legal action for his rights of inheritance)
2.1.204 **attorneys-general** legal representatives
2.1.204 **sue** make a legal claim for
2.1.205 **livery** possession of lands (granted by the king to his nobles under the feudal system)
2.1.205 **offered homage** (the act of homage required upon the restoration of lands to their heir)
2.1.212 **by the while** nearby in the meantime
2.1.214 **by…understood** i.e. it should be understood about bad courses
2.1.215 **events** outcomes

Bid him repair to us to Ely House
To see this business. Tomorrow next
We will for Ireland, and 'tis time, I trow.
And we create, in absence of ourself,   220
Our uncle York Lord Governor of England;
For he is just, and always loved us well.
Come on, our Queen; tomorrow must we part.
Be merry, for our time of stay is short.

    [*Flourish.*] *Exeunt* [*all but Northumberland, Willoughby,
    and Ross*]

NORTHUMBERLAND   Well, lords, the Duke of Lancaster is dead.   225

ROSS   And living too, for now his son is Duke.

WILLOUGHBY   Barely in title, not in revenues.

NORTHUMBERLAND   Richly in both, if justice had her right.

ROSS   My heart is great, but it must break with silence
Ere't be disburdened with a liberal tongue.   230

NORTHUMBERLAND   Nay, speak thy mind, and let him ne'er speak
    more
That speaks thy words again to do thee harm.

WILLOUGHBY   Tends that thou wouldst speak to the Duke of
    Hereford?
If it be so, out with it boldly, man.
Quick is mine ear to hear of good towards him.   235

ROSS   No good at all that I can do for him,
Unless you call it good to pity him,
Bereft and gelded of his patrimony.

NORTHUMBERLAND   Now afore God, 'tis shame such wrongs are
    borne
In him, a royal prince, and many more   240
Of noble blood in this declining land.
The King is not himself, but basely led
By flatterers; and what they will inform

2.1.217 **repair** make his way
2.1.218 **see** attend to
2.1.219 **trow** think
2.1.229 **great** full of emotion, angry

2.1.230 **liberal** unrestrained
2.1.233 **Tends…to** does what you would
    speak concern
2.1.235 **Quick** eager, impatient

Merely in hate 'gainst any of us all,
That will the King severely prosecute, 245
'Gainst us, our lives, our children, and our heirs.

ROSS   The commons hath he pilled with grievous taxes,
And quite lost their hearts. The nobles hath he fined
For ancient quarrels, and quite lost their hearts.

WILLOUGHBY   And daily new exactions are devised, 250
As blanks, benevolences, and I wot not what.
But what, a' God's name, doth become of this?

NORTHUMBERLAND   Wars hath not wasted it, for warred he hath
        not,
But basely yielded upon compromise
That which his noble ancestors achieved with blows. 255
More hath he spent in peace than they in wars.

ROSS   The Earl of Wiltshire hath the realm in farm.

WILLOUGHBY   The King's grown bankrupt like a broken man.

NORTHUMBERLAND   Reproach and dissolution hangeth over him.

ROSS   He hath not money for these Irish wars, 260
His burdenous taxations notwithstanding,
But by the robbing of the banished Duke.

NORTHUMBERLAND   His noble kinsman. Most degenerate King!
But, lords, we hear this fearful tempest sing,
Yet seek no shelter to avoid the storm. 265
We see the wind sit sore upon our sails,
And yet we strike not, but securely perish.

ROSS   We see the very wreck that we must suffer,
And unavoided is the danger now
For suffering so the causes of our wreck. 270

2.1.244 **Merely in** purely out of
2.1.245 **That** i.e. which accusation
2.1.247 **commons** people (as distinct from the nobility of gentry)
2.1.247 **pilled** plundered
2.1.249 **ancient** former, long-past
2.1.251 **blanks** (the *blank charters* of 1.4.47)
2.1.251 **benevolences** forced loans
2.1.251 **wot** know

2.1.254–5 **But…blows** (alluding to the cession of Brest to the Duke of Brittany)
2.1.257 **farm** lease (as in 1.4.44)
2.1.258 **broken** financially ruined
2.1.267 **strike** lower the sails; deliver blows
2.1.267 **securely** in our over-confidence
2.1.268 **wreck** follows the tempest and shipwreck imagery (with a possible pun on *rack*)
2.1.269 **unavoided** unavoidable
2.1.270 **suffering** enduring

NORTHUMBERLAND   Not so. Even through the hollow eyes of death,
    I spy life peering, but I dare not say
    How near the tidings of our comfort is.

WILLOUGHBY   Nay, let us share thy thoughts as thou dost ours.

ROSS   Be confident to speak, Northumberland.   275
    We three are but thyself, and speaking so,
    Thy words are but as thoughts. Therefore be bold.

NORTHUMBERLAND   Then thus. I have from le Port Blanc,
    A bay in Brétagne, received intelligence
    That Harry Duke of Hereford, Reinold Lord Cobham,   280
    Thomas, son and heir to the Earl of Arundel
    That late broke from the Duke of Exeter,
    His brother, Archbishop late of Canterbury,
    Sir Thomas Erpingham, Sir Thomas Ramston,
    Sir John Norbery, Sir Robert Waterton, and Francis Coint;   285
    All these well furnished by the Duke of Brétagne
    With eight tall ships, three thousand men of war,
    Are making hither with all due expedience,
    And shortly mean to touch our northern shore.
    Perhaps they had ere this, but that they stay   290
    The first departing of the King for Ireland.
    If then we shall shake off our slavish yoke,
    Imp out our drooping country's broken wing,
    Redeem from broking pawn the blemished crown,
    Wipe off the dust that hides our sceptre's gilt,   295
    And make high majesty look like itself,
    Away with me in post to Ravenspurgh.
    But if you faint, as fearing to do so,

2.1.271 **eyes** eye-sockets
2.1.279 **Brétagne** French province known as Brittany in English
2.1.281 **Thomas…Arundel** (A line not in early texts. As Shakespeare's source states, it was Arundel's son who 'broke from' Exeter. Evidently, a line has been lost, which editors approximately restore.)
2.1.282 **late broke** recently quarrelled
2.1.283 **His** i.e. the Earl of Arundel's
2.1.287 **men of war** fighting men

2.1.288 **expedience** haste
2.1.290–1 **stay…departing** first wait for the departure
2.1.293 **Imp out** engraft new feathers onto (from falconry)
2.1.294 **broking pawn** i.e. the possession of those who lease the right to gather taxes
2.1.297 **in post** with speed
2.1.297 **Ravenspurgh** (then an important port on the River Humber)
2.1.298 **faint** are faint-hearted

Stay, and be secret, and myself will go.

ROSS   To horse, to horse! Urge doubts to them that fear.   300

WILLOUGHBY   Hold out my horse, and I will first be there.

Exeunt

2.2

Sc. 6   *Enter the Queen, Bushy, Bagot*

BUSHY   Madam, your majesty is too much sad.
You promised when you parted with the King
To lay aside life-harming heaviness
And entertain a cheerful disposition.

QUEEN   To please the King I did; to please myself   5
I cannot do it. Yet I know no cause
Why I should welcome such a guest as grief,
Save bidding farewell to so sweet a guest
As my sweet Richard. Yet again, methinks
Some unborn sorrow, ripe in fortune's womb,   10
Is coming towards me; and my inward soul
At nothing trembles, with something it grieves
More than with parting from my lord the King.

BUSHY   Each substance of a grief hath twenty shadows
Which shows like grief itself but is not so;   15
For sorrow's eye, glazèd with blinding tears,
Divides one thing entire to many objects,
Like perspectives, which rightly gazed upon
Show nothing but confusion; eyed awry,
Distinguish form. So your sweet majesty,   20

2.1.301 **Hold out my horse** if my horse lasts out

Sc. 6 2.2.3 **life-harming heaviness** (from Ecclesiasticus 30:23: 'as for sorrow and heaviness, drive it from thee: for heaviness hath slain many a man, and bringeth no profit'; sorrow was also thought to be a waste of blood)
2.2.12 **something** (accented on the second syllable)
2.2.14–15 **Each...so** i.e. a single real grief gives rise to many illusory ones

2.2.18 **perspectives** pictures with a hidden subject which is distorted or unnoticed when viewed normally, but which can be seen when viewed from an angle or in a given way; (as suggested in 2.2.16–17) crystals which are cut to show distinct refracted images on their various facets. Accented on the first and third syllables.
2.2.18 **rightly** directly; properly
2.2.20 **Distinguish form** show distinct shapes

Looking awry upon your lord's departure,
Find shapes of grief more than himself to wail,
Which, looked on as it is, is naught but shadows
Of what it is not. Then, thrice-gracious Queen,
More than your lord's departure weep not. More is not seen,   25
Or if it be, 'tis with false sorrow's eye,
Which for things true weeps things imaginary.

QUEEN   It may be so; but yet my inward soul
Persuades me it is otherwise. Howe'er it be,
I cannot but be sad: so heavy-sad   30
As thought—on thinking on no thought I think—
Makes me with heavy nothing faint and shrink.

BUSHY   'Tis nothing but conceit, my gracious lady.

QUEEN   'Tis nothing less: conceit is still derived
From some forefather grief; mine is not so;   35
For nothing hath begot my something grief—
Or something hath the nothing that I grieve—
'Tis in reversion that I do possess,
But what it is that is not yet known what,
I cannot name; 'tis nameless woe, I wot.   40

        [*Enter Green*]

GREEN   God save your majesty, and well met, gentlemen.
I hope the King is not yet shipped for Ireland.

QUEEN   Why hop'st thou so? 'Tis better hope he is;
For his designs crave haste, his haste good hope.

2.2.21 **awry** from an angle; wrongly
2.2.22 **shapes…himself** continues the
metaphors of the hidden image (mainly)
and the multiplying crystal (also)
2.2.22 **shapes** images (implying
'appearance, illusions')
2.2.22 **wail** bewail
2.2.23 **Which** (referring back to *shapes of
grief*)
2.2.23–4 **shadows…not** i.e. imitations of
real grief
2.2.27 **for** as if they were; or instead of
2.2.30 **heavy** (often describes a pregnancy
and so perhaps here anticipates *conceit*—
see note to 2.2.33—and 'begot' in 2.2.36)

2.2.33 **conceit** as affliction of the mind,
imaginary idea. Perhaps also 'fanciful
imagery', but not taken up in this sense
in 2.2.34, where there may be a quibble
on 'conceived child'.
2.2.34 **nothing less** i.e. anything but *conceit*
2.2.34 **still** always
2.2.37 **something…grieve** i.e. the grief
which I feel over nothing actually
appertains elsewhere
2.2.38 **in reversion** by succession at a later
date
2.2.38 **possess** come into possession
2.2.43 **'Tis better** it is better to
2.2.44 **crave** greatly need

Then wherefore dost thou hope he is not shipped?   45

GREEN   That he, our hope, might have retired his power,
And driven into despair an enemy's hope,
Who strongly hath set footing in this land.
The banished Bolingbroke repeals himself,
And with uplifted arms is safe arrived   50
At Ravenspurgh.

QUEEN   Now God in heaven forbid!

GREEN   Ah, madam, 'tis too true! And, that is worse,
The Lord Northumberland, his son young Harry Percy,
The Lords of Ross, Beaumont, and Willoughby,
With all their powerful friends, are fled to him.   55

BUSHY   Why have you not proclaimed Northumberland
And all the rest revolted faction-traitors?

GREEN   We have, whereupon the Earl of Worcester
Hath broke his staff, resigned his stewardship,
And all the household servants fled with him   60
To Bolingbroke.

QUEEN   So, Green, thou art the midwife to my woe,
And Bolingbroke my sorrow's dismal heir.
Now hath my soul brought forth her prodigy,
And I, a gasping new-delivered mother,   65
Have woe to woe, sorrow to sorrow joined.

BUSHY   Despair not, madam.

QUEEN   Who shall hinder me?
I will despair, and be at enmity
With cozening hope. He is a flatterer,
A parasite, a keeper-back of death,   70
Who gently would dissolve the bonds of life,

2.2.46 **retired his power** brought back
his forces
2.2.49 **repeals** recalls from exile
2.2.50 **arms** weapons
2.2.52 **that** what
2.2.57 **rest** rest of the
2.2.59 **broke his staff** (symbolically
resigning his office)

2.2.59 **his stewardship** (The Earl of
Worcester was lord steward of the King's
household (2.2.60).)
2.2.62–5 **So…mother** (develops the
imagery of 2.2.10–12 and 2.2.30–6)
2.2.64 **prodigy** monstrous birth; portent
2.2.69 **cozening** cheating
2.2.71 **Who** i.e. death

Which false hope lingers in extremity.

[*Enter York, wearing a gorget*]

GREEN   Here comes the Duke of York.

QUEEN   With signs of war about his agèd neck.
O, full of careful business are his looks!   75
Uncle, for heaven's sake, speak comfortable words.

YORK   Should I do so, I should belie my thoughts.
Comfort's in heaven, and we are on the earth,
Where nothing lives but crosses, cares, and grief.
Your husband, he is gone to save far off,   80
Whilst others come to make him lose at home.
Here am I left to underprop his land,
Who, weak with age, cannot support myself.
Now comes the sick hour that his surfeit made.
Now shall he try his friends that flattered him.   85

Enter a [*Servingman*]

SERVINGMAN   My lord, your son was gone before I came.

YORK   He was? Why so, go all which way it will:
The nobles they are fled; the commons they are cold,
And will, I fear, revolt on Hereford's side.
Sirrah, get thee to Pleshey, to my sister Gloucester.   90
Bid her send me presently a thousand pound.—
Hold; take my ring.

SERVINGMAN   My lord, I had forgot to tell your lordship:
Today as I came by I callèd there—
But I shall grieve you to report the rest.   95

YORK   What is't, knave?

SERVINGMAN   An hour before I came, the Duchess died.

2.2.72 **lingers** prolongs
2.2.72 **in extremity** to the utmost; in the
  last moment of life
2.2.72.1 *gorget* piece of armour protecting
  the throat
2.2.75 **careful** anxious (perhaps also 'full
  of grief')
2.2.75 **business** preoccupation, anxiety,
  urgency

2.2.76 **comfortable** comforting
2.2.79 **crosses** misfortunes
2.2.85 **try** put to the test
2.2.90 **sister** i.e. sister-in-law
2.2.91 **presently** immediately
2.2.92 **ring** i.e. signet ring, which the
  servant takes as proof that he comes from
  the Duke of York

YORK   God for his mercy, what a tide of woes
         Comes rushing on this woeful land at once!
         I know not what to do. I would to God,   100
         So my untruth had not provoked him to it,
         The King had cut off my head with my brother's.
         What, are there no posts dispatched for Ireland?
         How shall we do for money for these wars?
         [*To the Queen*] Come, sister—cousin I would say—pray   105
         pardon me.
         [*To the Servingman*] Go, fellow, get thee home; provide
         some carts,
         And bring away the armour that is there.   [*Exit Servingman*]
         Gentlemen, will you go muster men?
         If I know how or which way to order these affairs
         Thus disorderly thrust into my hands,   110
         Never believe me. Both are my kinsmen,
         T'one is my sovereign, whom both my oath
         And duty bids defend; t'other again
         Is my kinsman, whom the King hath wronged,
         Whom conscience and my kindred bids to right.   115
         Well, somewhat we must do. [*To the Queen*] Come, cousin,
         I'll dispose of you.
         [*To Bushy, Bagot, and Green*] Gentlemen, go muster up your men,
         And meet me presently at Berkeley.
         I should to Pleshey too, but time will not permit.   120
         All is uneven,
         And every thing is left at six and seven.
                 Exeunt Duke [of York], Queen, manent Bushy and Green
BUSHY   The wind sits fair for news to go for Ireland,
         But none returns. For us to levy power

2.2.101 **So** provided that
2.2.101 **untruth** disloyalty
2.2.102 **my head** (*my* is emphatic)
2.2.103 **posts** fast messages
2.2.105 **sister** (the Duchess's death is
         uppermost in York's mind)
2.2.117 **dispose of** make arrangements for

2.2.118 **Gentlemen** (probably here
         pronounced as two syllables: 'gentl'men')
2.2.119 **presently** directly
2.2.122 **six and seven** at sixes and sevens,
         in confusion
2.2.123 **sits fair** blows from a favourable
         direction

Proportionable to the enemy is all unpossible. 125

GREEN   Besides, our nearness to the King in love,
Is near the hate of those love not the King.

BAGOT   And that's the wav'ring commons; for their love
Lies in their purses, and whoso empties them
By so much fills their hearts with deadly hate. 130

BUSHY   Wherein the King stands generally condemned.

BAGOT   If judgement lie in them, then so do we,
Because we ever have been near the King.

GREEN   Well, I will for refuge straight to Bristol Castle.
The Earl of Wiltshire is already there. 135

BUSHY   Thither will I with you, for little office
Will the hateful commoners perform for us,
Except like curs to tear us all to pieces.
[*To Bagot*] Will you go along with us?

BAGOT   No, I will to Ireland, to his majesty. 140
Farewell. If hearts' presages be not vain,
We three here part that ne'er shall meet again.

BUSHY   That's as York thrives to beat back Bolingbroke.

GREEN   Alas, poor Duke, the task he undertakes
Is numb'ring sands, and drinking oceans dry. 145
Where one on his side fights, thousands will fly.

[BAGOT]   Farewell at once, for once, for all, and ever.

BUSHY   Well, we may meet again.

BAGOT   I fear me never.
[*Exeunt Bagot at one door, Bushy and Greene at the other*]

2.3

Sc. 7   *Enter* [*Bolingbroke Duke of*] *Hereford, and Northumberland*

BOLINGBROKE   How far is it, my lord, to Berkeley now?

2.2.125 **Proportionable** proportional
2.2.126 **love** i.e. his affection
2.2.127 **Is near** implies
2.2.132 **lie in them** i.e. is in the people's hands
2.2.136 **office** service
2.2.137 **hateful** full of hate; odious

2.2.141 **presages** (accented on the second syllable)
2.2.143 **That's** as that depends on whether
2.2.143 **thrives to beat** succeeds in beating
2.2.145 **numb'ring...dry** (proverbial expressions for attempting the impossible)

NORTHUMBERLAND   Believe me, noble lord,
   I am a stranger here in Gloucestershire.
   These high wild hills and rough uneven ways
   Draws out our miles and makes them wearisome;   5
   And yet your fair discourse hath been as sugar,
   Making the hard way sweet and delectable.
   But I bethink me what a weary way
   From Ravenspurgh to Cotswold will be found,
   In Ross and Willoughby, wanting your company,   10
   Which I protest hath very much beguiled
   The tediousness and process of my travel.
   But theirs is sweetened with the hope to have
   The present benefit which I possess;
   And hope to joy is little less in joy   15
   Than hope enjoyed. By this the weary lords
   Shall make their way seem short as mine hath done
   By sight of what I have: your noble company.

BOLINGBROKE   Of much less value is my company
   Than your good words. But who comes here?   20

   Enter Harry Percy

NORTHUMBERLAND   It is my son young Harry Percy,
   Sent from my brother Worcester, whencesoever.
   Harry, how fares your uncle?

HARRY PERCY   I had thought, my lord, to have learned his health
   of you.

NORTHUMBERLAND   Why, is he not with the Queen?   25

HARRY PERCY   No, my good lord; he hath forsook the court,
   Broken his staff of office and dispersed
   The household of the King.

NORTHUMBERLAND   What was his reason?
   He was not so resolved when last we spoke together.

HARRY PERCY   Because your lordship was proclaimèd traitor.   30
   But he, my lord, is gone to Ravenspurgh,

Sc. 7 2.3.7 **delectable** (accented on the first and third syllables)
2.3.10 **In** by
2.3.11 **beguiled** whiled away
2.3.12 **tediousness and process** tedious process
2.3.15 **to joy** of enjoying; of being joyful
2.3.22 **whencesoever** wherever he may be

To offer service to the Duke of Hereford,
And sent me over by Berkeley to discover
What power the Duke of York had levied there,
Then with directions to repair to Ravenspurgh.   35

NORTHUMBERLAND   Have you forgot the Duke of Hereford, boy?

HARRY PERCY   No, my good lord, for that is not forgot
Which ne'er I did remember. To my knowledge,
I never in my life did look on him.

NORTHUMBERLAND   Then learn to know him now: this is the Duke.   40

HARRY PERCY [*to Bolingbroke*]   My gracious lord, I tender you
      my service,
Such as it is, being tender, raw, and young,
Which elder days shall ripen and confirm
To more approvèd service and desert.

BOLINGBROKE   I thank thee, gentle Percy, and be sure   45
I count myself in nothing else so happy
As in a soul rememb'ring my good friends;
And as my fortune ripens with thy love,
It shall be still thy true love's recompense.
My heart this covenant makes; my hand thus seals it.   50

      [*He clasps Harry Percy's hand*]

NORTHUMBERLAND [*to Harry Percy*]   How far is it to Berkeley,
      and what stir
Keeps good old York there with his men of war?

HARRY PERCY   There stands the castle, by yon tuft of trees,
Manned with three hundred men, as I have heard,
And in it are the Lords of York, Berkeley, and Seymour,   55
None else of name and noble estimate.

      [*Enter Ross and Willoughby*]

NORTHUMBERLAND   Here come the Lords of Ross and Willoughby,
Bloody with spurring, fiery red with haste.

2.3.44 **more approvèd** better tested
2.3.51 **stir** state of action
2.3.53 **tuft** cluster, clump
2.3.56 **name** (synonymous with *noble estimate*)

2.3.56 **estimate** reputation
2.3.58 **Bloody** (overspurring drew blood from a horse)
2.3.58 **fiery red** (in complexion)

BOLINGBROKE   Welcome, my lords. I wot your love pursues
  A banished traitor. All my treasury   60
  Is yet but unfelt thanks, which, more enriched,
  Shall be your love and labour's recompense.

ROSS   Your presence makes us rich, most noble lord.

WILLOUGHBY   And far surmounts our labour to attain it.

BOLINGBROKE   Evermore thank's the exchequer of the poor,   65
  Which, till my infant fortune comes to years,
  Stands for my bounty. But who comes here?

    [Enter Berkeley]

NORTHUMBERLAND   It is my lord of Berkeley, as I guess.

BERKELEY   My lord of Hereford, my message is to you.

BOLINGBROKE   My lord, my answer is to 'Lancaster';   70
  And I am come to seek that name in England,
  And I must find that title in your tongue
  Before I make reply to aught you say.

BERKELEY   Mistake me not, my lord; 'tis not my meaning
  To raze one title of your honour out.   75
  To you, my lord, I come—what lord you will—
  From the most gracious regent of this land,
  The Duke of York, to know what pricks you on
  To take advantage of the absent time,
  And fright our native peace with self-borne arms?   80

    [Enter Duke of York]

BOLINGBROKE   I shall not need transport my words by you.
  Here comes his grace in person. My noble uncle!

    [He kneels]

YORK   Show me thy humble heart, and not thy knee,
  Whose duty is deceivable and false.

2.3.59 **wot** know
2.3.61 **unfelt** i.e. manifest only
  in words
2.3.61 **which** (may refer to 'treasury' or
  'thanks')
2.3.65 **Evermore** always
2.3.65 **thank's** gratitude is
2.3.65 **exchequer** treasury, wealth
2.3.66 **to years** of age

2.3.70 **my…'Lancaster'** i.e. I only reply to
  my title of Lancaster
2.3.75 **title** (perhaps quibbling on *tittle*)
2.3.78 **pricks you on** incites you
2.3.79 **absent time** time in absence
2.3.80 **self-borne** borne for oneself, not
  for the king; *self-born* i.e. arising through
  our native conflicts
2.3.84 **deceivable** deceptive

BOLINGBROKE   My gracious uncle—   85

YORK   Tut tut, grace me no grace, nor uncle me no uncle.
  I am no traitor's uncle, and that word 'grace'
  In an ungracious mouth is but profane.
  Why have those banished and forbidden legs
  Dared once to touch a dust of England's ground?   90
  But then more why: why have they dared to march
  So many miles upon her peaceful bosom,
  Frighting her pale-faced villages with war
  And ostentation of despisèd arms?
  Com'st thou because the anointed King is hence?   95
  Why, foolish boy, the King is left behind,
  And in my loyal bosom lies his power.
  Were I but now the lord of such hot youth
  As when brave Gaunt, thy father, and myself
  Rescued the Black Prince, that young Mars of men,   100
  From forth the ranks of many thousand French,
  O then how quickly should this arm of mine,
  Now prisoner to the palsy, chastise thee
  And minister correction to thy fault!

BOLINGBROKE   My gracious uncle, let me know my fault.   105
  On what condition stands it, and wherein?

YORK   Even in condition of the worst degree:
  In gross rebellion and detested treason.
  Thou art a banished man, and here art come,
  Before the expiration of thy time,   110
  In braving arms against thy sovereign.

BOLINGBROKE   As I was banished, I was banished Hereford;
  But as I come, I come for Lancaster.
  And, noble uncle, I beseech your grace
  Look on my wrongs with an indifferent eye.   115

2.3.90 **dust** speck
2.3.94 **ostentation** ostentatious display
2.3.94 **despisèd** despicable
2.3.101 **From forth** out of
2.3.103 **chastise** (accented on the first
  syllable)
2.3.104 **correction** punishment

2.3.106 **condition** characteristic;
  circumstances
2.3.108 **detested** detestable
2.3.111 **braving** defiant
2.3.113 **for** as
2.3.115 **wrongs** i.e. wrongs suffered
2.3.115 **indifferent** impartial

You are my father, for methinks in you
I see old Gaunt alive. O then, my father,
Will you permit that I shall stand condemned
A wandering vagabond, my rights and royalties
Plucked from my arms perforce; and given away   120
To upstart unthrifts? Wherefore was I born?
If that my cousin King be King in England,
It must be granted I am Duke of Lancaster.
You have a son, Aumerle, my noble cousin.
Had you first died, and he been thus trod down,   125
He should have found his uncle Gaunt a father
To rouse his wrongs and chase them to the bay.
I am denied to sue my livery here,
And yet my letters patents give me leave.
My father's goods are all distrained and sold,   130
And these, and all, are all amiss employed.
What would you have me do? I am a subject,
And I challenge law. Attorneys are denied me;
And therefore personally I lay my claim
To my inheritance of free descent.   135

NORTHUMBERLAND [*to York*]   The noble Duke hath been too
      much abused.

ROSS [*to York*]   It stands your grace upon to do him right.

WILLOUGHBY [*to York*]   Base men by his endowments are made
      great.

YORK   My lords of England, let me tell you this:
I have had feeling of my cousin's wrongs,   140
And laboured all I could to do him right.
But in this kind to come—in braving arms,
Be his own carver, and cut out his way

2.3.121 **unthrifts** spendthrifts
2.3.127 **rouse** startle from cover. The line's
  imagery is from hunting.
2.3.128 **sue my livery** (see notes to 2.1.204
  and 2.1.205)
2.3.130 **distrained** seized
2.3.133 **challenge** demand as a right
2.3.135 **of** by
2.3.137 **It…upon** it is incumbent upon
  your grace

2.3.138 **his endowments** the property that
  he has (involuntarily) endowed
2.3.142 **kind** manner
2.3.143 **Be…carver** i.e. take what he can get
2.3.143 **carver** one who carves at the table
  (the usual sense); one who shapes things
  by carving (a quibbling sense which York
  develops)

To find out right with wrong—it may not be.
And you that do abet him in this kind   145
Cherish rebellion, and are rebels all.

NORTHUMBERLAND   The noble Duke hath sworn his coming is
But for his own, and for the right of that
We all have strongly sworn to give him aid;
And let him never see joy that breaks that oath.   150

YORK   Well, well, I see the issue of these arms.
I cannot mend it, I must needs confess,
Because my power is weak and all ill left.
But if I could, by Him that gave me life,
I would attach you all, and make you stoop   155
Unto the sovereign mercy of the King.
But since I cannot, be it known to you
I do remain as neuter. So fare you well—
Unless you please to enter in the castle
And there repose you for this night.   160

BOLINGBROKE   An offer, uncle, that we will accept.
But we must win your grace to go with us
To Bristol Castle, which they say is held
By Bushy, Bagot, and their complices,
The caterpillars of the commonwealth,   165
Which I have sworn to weed and pluck away.

YORK   It may be I will go with you; but yet I'll pause,
For I am loath to break our country's laws.
Nor friends nor foes to me welcome you are.
Things past redress are now with me past care.   *Exeunt.* 170

2.3.144 **find out** discover the shape of
(developing the carving image)
2.3.144 **right** (quibbling on 'his right' and
'what is right')
2.3.146 **Cherish** foster
2.3.151 **issue** consequence
2.3.152 **mend** remedy
2.3.153 **power** military strength
2.3.153 **all ill left** everything is left in
disorder; or left utterly inadequate
2.3.155 **attach** unrest

2.3.158 **as neuter** neutral
2.3.164 **complices** accomplices
2.3.165 **caterpillars** i.e. devourers
2.3.166 **weed** remove (as of vermin, not
plants)
2.3.167 **yet I'll pause** for now I will delay
acting
2.3.169 **Nor...nor** neither as...nor as
2.3.170 **Things...care** (of proverbial
origin)

2.4

Sc. 8 *Enter the Earl of Salisbury and a Welsh Captain*

WELSH CAPTAIN   My lord of Salisbury, we have stayed ten days,
  And hardly kept our countrymen together,
  And yet we hear no tidings from the King;
  Therefore we will disperse ourselves. Farewell.

SALISBURY   Stay yet another day, thou trusty Welshman.   5
  The King reposeth all his confidence in thee.

WELSH CAPTAIN   'Tis thought the King is dead. We will not stay.
  The bay trees in our country are all withered,
  And meteors fright the fixèd stars of heaven.
  The pale-faced moon looks bloody on the earth,   10
  And lean-looked prophets whisper fearful change.
  Rich men look sad, and ruffians dance and leap;
  The one in fear to lose what they enjoy,
  The other to enjoy by rage and war.
  These signs forerun the death or fall of kings.   15
  Farewell. Our countrymen are gone and fled,
  As well assurèd Richard their king is dead.   [*Exit*]

SALISBURY   Ah, Richard, with the eyes of heavy mind
  I see thy glory, like a shooting star,
  Fall to the base earth from the firmament.   20
  Thy sun sets weeping in the lowly west,
  Witnessing storms to come, woe, and unrest.
  Thy friends are fled to wait upon thy foes,
  And crossly to thy good all fortune goes.   [*Exit*]

Sc. 8 2.4.1 **stayed** waited, delayed
2.4.3 **yet** still
2.4.8–10 **The…earth** (Holinshed records the first of these omens (though as observed in England, not Wales); the others are poetic commonplaces.)
2.4.11 **lean-looked** lean-faced
2.4.11 **prophets** prognosticators (not seen as divinely inspired)
2.4.14 **to enjoy** hoping to profit
2.4.14 **rage** violence

2.4.17 **As** being
2.4.21 **Thy…west** (possibly suggesting Richard's emblem, a sun showing between clouds)
2.4.21 **weeping** (perhaps 'red-eyed'; according to one proverb, a red sunset predicted rain; but see also previous note)
2.4.22 **Witnessing** giving evidence of
2.4.24 **crossly** adversely

3.1

Sc. 9 *Enter [Bolingbroke] Duke of Hereford, York,*
        Northumberland, [Ross, Harry Percy, and Willoughby]

BOLINGBROKE   Bring forth these men.

   [Enter] Bushy and Green, [guarded as] prisoners

   Bushy and Green, I will not vex your souls,
   Since presently your souls must part your bodies,
   With too much urging your pernicious lives,
   For 'twere no charity. Yet to wash your blood   5
   From off my hands, here in the view of men
   I will unfold some causes of your deaths.
   You have misled a prince, a royal king,
   A happy gentleman in blood and lineaments,
   By you unhappied and disfigured clean.   10
   You have, in manner, with your sinful hours
   Made a divorce betwixt his queen and him,
   Broke the possession of a royal bed,
   And stained the beauty of a fair queen's cheeks
   With tears, drawn from her eyes by your foul wrongs.   15
   Myself, a prince by fortune of my birth,
   Near to the King in blood, and near in love
   Till you did make him misinterpret me,
   Have stooped my neck under your injuries,
   And sighed my English breath in foreign clouds,   20
   Eating the bitter bread of banishment,
   Whilst you have fed upon my signories,

Sc. 9 3.1.2 **vex** afflict
3.1.3 **presently** immediately
3.1.3 **part** part from
3.1.4 **too...lives** over-asserting
how destructive your lives have been
3.1.10 **clean** utterly
3.1.11 **in manner** in effect
3.1.12 **divorce** division (not 'dissolution of
marriage')
3.1.13 **Broke...bed** i.e. violated the
royal marriage contract. This seems

to imply that Bushy and Greene
had homosexual relationships
with Richard.
3.1.16 **Myself** I myself
3.1.17 **Near** closely related
3.1.20 **in foreign clouds** into the gloomy
foreign air; in clouds foreign to the air
surrounding them
3.1.21 **bread of banishment** 'bread of
affliction' in biblical (2 Kings 22:27)
3.1.22 **signories** estates

Disparked my parks, and felled my forest woods,
From my own windows torn my household coat,
Razed out my impress, leaving me no sign,   25
Save men's opinions and my living blood,
To show the world I am a gentleman.
This and much more, much more than twice all this,
Condemns you to the death. See them delivered over
To execution and the hand of death.   30

BUSHY   More welcome is the stroke of death to me
   Than Bolingbroke to England. Lords, farewell.

GREEN   My comfort is that heaven will take our souls,
   And plague injustice with the pains of hell.

BOLINGBROKE   My lord Northumberland, see them dispatched.   35
   [*Exit Northumberland, with Bushy and Green, guarded*]
   Uncle, you say the Queen is at your house.
   For God's sake fairly let her be entreated.
   Tell her I send to her my kind commends.
   Take special care my greetings be delivered.

YORK   A gentleman of mine I have dispatched   40
   With letters of your love to her at large.

BOLINGBROKE   Thanks, gentle uncle. Come, lords, away,
   To fight with Glyndŵr and his complices.
   A while to work, and after, holiday.   *Exeunt.*

3.1.23 **Disparked** i.e. put to other uses, much as tillage
3.1.23 **parks** enclosed hunting estates
3.1.23 **felled…woods** (Aristocrats preserved woods for revenue from timber in times of hardship.)
3.1.23 **felled** i.e. cleared to make way for agriculture
3.1.24 **torn my household coat** forcibly removed the stained glass bearing my coat-of-arms (with word-play in 'torn' and 'coat')
3.1.25 **Razed my impress** (a paraphrase of 3.1.24)

3.1.25 **impress** heraldic emblem
3.1.25 **sign** heraldic emblem; indication
3.1.26 **opinions** esteem
3.1.34 **plague injustice** inflict retribution on the unjust
3.1.37 **fairly** courteously
3.1.37 **entreated** treated
3.1.38 **commends** greetings
3.1.41 **of…large** expressing fully your kindness towards her
3.1.43 **Glyndŵr** (the character appears in *1 Henry IV*)

3.2

Sc. 10 [*Flourish.*] *Enter* [*with drums and colours*] *the King,*
        Aumerle, Carlisle, and [*soldiers*]

KING RICHARD   Barkloughly Castle call they this at hand?

AUMERLE   Yea, my lord. How brooks your grace the air
After late tossing on the breaking seas?

KING RICHARD   Needs must I like it well. I weep for joy
To stand upon my kingdom once again.   5
Dear earth, I do salute thee with my hand.
Though rebels wound thee with their horses' hoofs.
As a long-parted mother with her child
Plays fondly with her tears, and smiles in meeting,
So, weeping, smiling, greet I thee my earth,   10
And do thee favours with my royal hands.
Feed not thy sovereign's foe, my gentle earth,
Nor with thy sweets comfort his ravenous sense;
But let thy spiders that suck up thy venom
And heavy-gaited toads lie in their way,   15
Doing annoyance to the treacherous feet
Which with usurping steps do trample thee.
Yield stinging nettles to mine enemies,
And, when they from thy bosom pluck a flower,
Guard it, I pray thee, with a lurking adder,   20
Whose double tongue may with a mortal touch
Throw death upon thy sovereign's enemies.
Mock not my senseless conjuration, lords.

Sc. 10 3.2.0 *drums and colours* i.e.
    formal procession led by drummers
    and standard-bearers
3.2.2 **brooks** enjoys
3.2.3 **late** recent
3.2.6 **salute** (perhaps implying 'wish
    health to'; the king's touch was
    popularly thought to have healing
    properties)
3.2.8 **long-parted mother with** mother
    long parted from
3.2.9 **Plays fondly** i.e. dotingly indulges
    herself
3.2.11 **favours** kindly and favourable acts
3.2.13 **sweets** delights

3.2.13 **ravenous** (pronounced as two
    syllables)
3.2.13 **sense** senses; sensuality
3.2.14 **let...venom** (It was thought that
    spiders were poisonous, and that they
    drew their venom from the earth.)
3.2.15 **heavy-gaited** slow-footed, sluggish
3.2.15 **toads** (also thought to be venomous)
3.2.16 **annoyance** harm
3.2.18 **Yield** bring forth
3.2.19–20 **And...adder** (The snake
    hidden below the flower was proverbial.)
3.2.21 **double** forked
3.2.23 **senseless** i.e. addressed to the
    (usually) insentient earth

This earth shall have a feeling, and these stones
Prove armèd soldiers ere her native king 25
Shall falter under foul rebellion's arms.

BISHOP OF CARLISLE   Fear not, my lord. That power that made
    you king
Hath power to keep you king in spite of all.
The means that heaven's yield must be embraced,
And not neglected; else heaven would, 30
And we will not heaven's offer we refuse—
The proffered means of succour and redress.

AUMERLE   He means, my lord, that we are too remiss,
Whilst Bolingbroke, through our security,
Grows strong and great in substance and in power. 35

KING RICHARD   Discomfortable cousin, know'st thou not
That, when the searching eye of heaven is hid
Behind the globe that lights the lower world,
Then thieves and robbers range abroad unseen
In murders and in outrage bloody here; 40
But when from under this terrestrial ball
He fires the proud tops of the eastern pines
And darts his light through every guilty hole,
Then murders, treasons and detested sins,
The cloak of night being plucked from off their backs, 45
Stand bare and naked trembling at themselves?
So when this thief, this traitor, Bolingbroke,
Who all this while hath revelled in the night
Whilst we were wand'ring with the Antipodes,

3.2.24–5 **these…soldiers** (recalling the legend of Cadmus, who sowed a monster's tooth in the ground, from which sprang *armèd soldiers*; there are also possible echoes of Job 5:23, and Luke 3:8 and 9:40)
3.2.25 **native** natural, rightful
3.2.30 **else** otherwise
3.2.30 **would** wishes
3.2.34 **security** overconfidence
3.2.36 **Discomfortable** disheartening
3.2.37 **eye of heaven** sun
3.2.37–8 **is hid…world** i.e. night-time in England when the moon supplies light

so that nefarious figures can commit evil acts while 'rang[ing] abroad unseen'
3.2.38 **globe** moon
3.2.38 **lower world** earthly, human world (as opposed to the heavenly one); 'the place of the damned' *OED*
3.2.40 **outrage** violent conduct
3.2.41 **terrestrial ball** moon
3.2.46 **themselves** i.e. their revealed wickedness
3.2.49 **with the Antipodes** amongst the Antipodeans (an exaggeration)

Shall see us rising in our throne, the east,   50
His treasons will sit blushing in his face,
Not able to endure the sight of day,
But, self-affrighted, tremble at his sin.
Not all the water in the rough rude sea
Can wash the balm off from a 'nointed king.   55
The breath of worldly men cannot depose
The deputy elected by the Lord.
For every man that Bolingbroke hath pressed
To lift shrewd steel against our golden crown,
God for his Richard hath in heavenly pay   60
A glorious angel. Then, if angels fight,
Weak men must fall; for heaven still guards the right.

> *Enter Salisbury*

Welcome, my lord. How far off lies your power?

SALISBURY Nor nea'er nor farther off, my gracious lord,
Than this weak arm. Discomfort guides my tongue,   65
And bids me speak of nothing but despair.
One day too late, I fear me, noble lord,
Hath clouded all thy happy days on earth.
O, call back yesterday, bid time return,
And thou shalt have twelve thousand fighting men.   70
Today, today, unhappy day too late,
Overthrows thy joys, friends, fortune, and thy state;
For all the Welshmen, hearing thou wert dead,
Are gone to Bolingbroke, dispersed, and fled.

AUMERLE Comfort, my liege. Why looks your grace so pale? 75

KING RICHARD But now the blood of twenty thousand men
Did triumph in my face, and they are fled;

3.2.50 **Shall…east** (the image implies Christ-like qualities)
3.2.54 **rude** turbulent
3.2.55 **balm** oil of consecration
3.2.57 **elected** chosen
3.2.58 **pressed** conscripted
3.2.59 **shrewd** harmful; wicked (also perhaps 'harsh' or 'sharp')
3.2.62 **still** always

3.2.63 **power** army (but in Salisbury's reply 'military strength')
3.2.64 **nea'er** nearer
3.2.67 **One day too late** i.e. you being one day too late
3.2.72 **Overthrows** (pronounced as two syllables)
3.2.72 **state** prosperity, power
3.2.76 **But now** a moment ago

And till so much blood thither come again,
Have I not reason to look pale and dead?
All souls that will be safe fly from my side,   80
For time hath set a blot upon my pride.

AUMERLE   Comfort, my liege. Remember who you are.

KING RICHARD   I had forgot myself. Am I not King?
Awake, thou coward majesty, thou sleep'st!
Is not the King's name twenty thousand names?   85
Arm, arm, my name! A puny subject strikes
At thy great glory. Look not to the ground,
Ye favourites of a king. Are we not high?
High be our thoughts. I know my uncle York
Hath power enough to serve our turn. But who comes here?   90

    Enter Scrope

SCROPE   More health and happiness betide my liege
Than can my care-tuned tongue deliver him.

KING RICHARD   Mine ear is open, and my heart prepared.
The worst is worldly loss thou canst unfold.
Say, is my kingdom lost? Why, 'twas my care,   95
And what loss is it to be rid of care?
Strives Bolingbroke to be as great as we?
Greater he shall not be. If he serve God,
We'll serve him too, and be his fellow so.
Revolt our subjects? That we cannot mend.   100
They break their faith to God as well as us.
Cry woe, destruction, ruin, and decay!
The worst is death, and death will have his day.

SCROPE   Glad am I that your highness is so armed
To bear the tidings of calamity,   105
Like an unseasonable stormy day,
Which makes the silver rivers drown their shores
As if the world were all dissolved to tears;
So high above his limits swells the rage

3.2.80 **will** wish to
3.2.92 **care-tuned** tuned to the key
  of sorrow: with a tune expressing
  sorrow
3.2.92 **deliver** communicate to
3.2.99 **fellow** equal
3.2.102 **Cry** i.e. though you may cry
3.2.109 **limits** bounds, banks

Of Bolingbroke, covering your fearful land   110
With hard bright steel, and hearts harder than steel.
White-beards have armed their thin and hairless scalps
Against thy majesty. Boys with women's voices
Strive to speak big and clap their female joints
In stiff unwieldy arms against thy crown.   115
Thy very beadsmen learn to bend their bows
Of double-fatal yew against thy state.
Yea, distaff-women manage rusty bills
Against thy seat. Both young and old rebel,
And all goes worse than I have power to tell.   120

KING RICHARD   Too well, too well thou tell'st a tale so ill.
Where is the Earl of Wiltshire? Where is Bagot?
What is become of Bushy? Where is Green?
That they have let the dangerous enemy
Measure our confines with such peaceful steps,   125
If we prevail, their heads shall pay for it:
I warrant they have made peace with Bolingbroke.

SCROPE   Peace have they made with him indeed, my lord.

KING RICHARD   O villains, vipers, damned without redemption!
Dogs easily won to fawn on any man!   130
Snakes in my heart-blood warmed, that sting my heart!
Three Judases, each one thrice worse than Judas!
Would they make peace? Terrible hell,
Make war upon their spotted souls for this.

SCROPE   Sweet love, I see, changing his property,   135

3.2.110 **fearful** full of fear
3.2.112 **thin** thin-haired
3.2.114 **big** deep, with full voice
3.2.114 **female** i.e. weak
3.2.115 **arms** armour
3.2.117 **double-fatal** (because (i) yew is poisonous; (ii) its wood was used to make bows)
3.2.118 **distaff-women** spinners. The *distaff* is the staff onto which spun thread is wound, and was a satirical example of a woman's weapon.
3.2.118 **manage** wield
3.2.118 **bills** (weapons with a blade or spiked axe on a long shaft)

3.2.119 **seat** throne
3.2.122 **Where is Bagot** (an inconsistency, for Bagot is not one of the 'three Judases' (3.2.132) who are dead)
3.2.125 **Measure our confines** travel over out territories
3.2.125 **peaceful** unopposed
3.2.129 **vipers...redemption** (perhaps suggested by Matthew 23:33)
3.2.129 **without** beyond
3.2.131 **Snakes...heart** (a proverbial image)
3.2.134 **spotted** stained, blemished
3.2.135 **his property** its distinctive quality

Turns to the sourest and most deadly hate.
Again uncurse their souls. Their peace is made
With heads and not with hands. Those whom you curse
Have felt the worst of death's destroying wound,
And lie full low, graved in the hollow ground.   140

AUMERLE   Is Bushy, Green, and the Earl of Wiltshire dead?

SCROPE   Ay, all of them at Bristol lost their heads.

AUMERLE   Where is the Duke my father with his power?

KING RICHARD   No matter where. Of comfort no man speak.
Let's talk of graves, of worms, and epitaphs,   145
Make dust our paper, and with rainy eyes
Write sorrow on the bosom of the earth.
Let's choose executors and talk of wills.—
And yet, not so, for what can we bequeath
Save our deposèd bodies to the ground?   150
Our lands, our lives, and all are Bolingbroke's;
And nothing can we call our own but death,
And that small model of the barren earth
Which serves as paste and cover to our bones.
For God's sake, let us sit upon the ground,   155
And tell sad stories of the death of kings—
How some have been deposed, some slain in war,
Some haunted by the ghosts they have deposed,
Some poisoned by their wives, some sleeping killed—
All murdered; for within the hollow crown   160
That rounds the mortal temples of a king
Keeps Death his court; and there the antic sits,
Scoffing his state and grinning at his pomp,
Allowing him a breath, a little scene,
To monarchize, be feared, and kill with looks,   165

3.2.140 **ground** (rhymes with *wound*)
3.2.146 **dust** ashes; earth
3.2.150 **deposèd** divested (both in general and in the sense 'dethroned')
3.2.153 **model** small-scale imitation, microcosm (i.e. the body); or mould, enveloping shape (i.e. the grave)
3.2.154 **paste** pastry; pie-lid (also known as a *coffin*)

3.2.161 **rounds** encircles
3.2.162 **antic** clown, jester
3.2.163 **his** i.e. the king's; not, as in 3.2.162, Death's
3.2.163 **state** regality
3.2.163 **grinning** (suggesting the expression of Death's emblem, the skull)

Infusing him with self and vain conceit,
As if this flesh which walls about our life
Were brass impregnable; and, humoured thus,
Comes at the last, and with a little pin
Bores through his castle wall; and farewell, king.   170
Cover your heads, and mock not flesh and blood
With solemn reverence. Throw away respect,
Tradition, form, and ceremonious duty,
For you have but mistook me all this while.
I live with bread, like you feel want,   175
Taste grief, need friends. Subjected thus,
How can you say to me I am a king?

BISHOP OF CARLISLE   My lord, wise men ne'er sit and wail their
  woes,
But presently prevent the ways to wail.
To fear the foe, since fear oppresseth strength,   180
Gives in your weakness strength unto your foe;
And so your follies fight against yourself.
Fear and be slain, no worse can come to fight;
And fight and die is death destroying death,
Where fearing dying pays death servile breath.   185

AUMERLE   My father hath a power. Enquire of him,
And learn to make a body of a limb.

KING RICHARD   Thou chid'st me well. Proud Bolingbroke, I come
To change blows with thee for our day of doom.
This ague-fit of fear is overblown.   190

3.2.168 **humoured thus** the king being
  this indulged; when Death has thus
  amused himself; Death being in this mood
3.2.170 **castle wall** i.e. flesh (as in 3.2.167)
3.2.171 **Cover your heads** replace your
  hats (i.e. do not do the 'reverence' of
  remaining bareheaded)
3.2.173 **form** formality, good behaviour
  (perhaps also rank)
3.2.173 **ceremonious** formal, customary
3.2.175 **with** by eating
3.2.176 **Subjected** liable; made a subject
3.2.179 **presently prevent** immediately
  debar

3.2.179 **to wail** state of woe
3.2.180 **oppresseth** suppresses
3.2.183 **and** i.e. and as a result
3.2.183 **to fight** in fighting
3.2.184 **fight...destroying death** i.e. to
  die fighting is to destroy death's power
  by death
3.2.185 **Where** whereas
3.2.186 **of** about
3.2.189 **change** exchange
3.2.189 **for...doom** to decide the
  outcome of our fateful day. (*Doom*
  rhymes with *come*.)

An easy task it is to win our own.
Say, Scrope, where lies our uncle with his power?
Speak sweetly, man, although thy looks be sour.

SCROOPE   Men judge by the complexion of the sky
The state and inclination of the day;   195
So may you by my dull and heavy eye.
My tongue hath but a heavier tale to say.
I play the torturer by small and small
To lengthen out the worst that must be spoken.
Your uncle York is joined with Bolingbroke,   200
And all your northern castles yielded up,
And all your southern gentlemen in arms
Upon his party.

KING RICHARD   Thou hast said enough.

[*To Aumerle*] Beshrew thee, cousin, which didst lead
me forth

Of that sweet way I was in to despair.   205
What say you now? What comfort have we now?
By heaven, I'll hate him everlastingly
That bids me be of comfort any more.
Go to Flint Castle; there I'll pine away.
A king, woe's slave, shall kingly woe obey.   210
That power I have, discharge, and let them go
To ear the land that hath some hope to grow;
For I have none. Let no man speak again
To alter this, for counsel is but vain.

AUMERLE   My liege, one word.   215

KING RICHARD   He does me double wrong
That wounds me with the flatteries of his tongue.
Discharge my followers. Let them hence away,
From Richard's night, to Bolingbroke's fair day.   [*Exeunt*]

3.2.196 **dull** gloomy
3.2.198 **by small and small** little by little
3.2.202 **gentlemen** gentry, men of rank
3.2.202 **in arms** are up in arms; who bear
weapons; or with coats of arms
3.2.203 **party** side
3.2.205 **Beshrew thee** woe to you (a mild
curse)
3.2.204 **which** who
3.2.204 **forth** out
3.2.210 **kingly** (in that it exacts
Richard's obedience; is Richard's,
a king's)
3.2.212 **ear** tell
3.2.212 **grow** flourish

3.3

Sc. 11   *Enter Bolingbroke Duke of Lancaster and Hereford, [the*
Duke of York, the Earl of Northumberland, [and soldiers,
with drum and colours]

BOLINGBROKE   So that by this intelligence we learn
The Welshmen are dispersed, and Salisbury
Is gone to meet the King, who lately landed
With some few private friends upon this coast.

NORTHUMBERLAND   The news is very fair and good, my lord.   5
Richard not far from hence hath hid his head.

YORK   It would beseem the Lord Northumberland
To say 'King Richard.' Alack the heavy day
When such a sacred king should hide his head!

NORTHUMBERLAND   Your grace mistakes. Only to be brief   10
Left I his title out.

YORK   The time hath been,
Would you have been so brief with him,
He would have been so brief to shorten you,
For taking so the head, your whole head's length.

BOLINGBROKE   Mistake not, uncle, further than you should.   15

YORK   Take not, good cousin, further than you should,
Lest you mistake the heavens are over our heads.

BOLINGBROKE   I know it, uncle, and oppose not myself
Against their will. But who comes here?

        Enter [Harry] Percy [and a trumpeter]

Welcome, Harry. What, will not this castle yield?   20

HARRY PERCY   The castle royally is manned, my lord,
Against thy entrance.

BOLINGBROKE   Royally?
Why, it contains no king.

HARRY PERCY   Yes, my good lord,

Sc. 11 3.3.1 **So that** so
3.3.6 **hid his head** taken shelter
3.3.11 **The time hath been** at one time
3.3.12 **Would you have** if you had
3.3.14 **taking so the head** omitting the
title so; acting without restraint.

3.3.17 **mistake** forget that;
or transgress. With the
latter *are ... heads* is a relative
clause ('which are ...').
3.3.18 **myself** (accented on *my*)

It doth contain a king: King Richard lies
Within the limits of yon lime and stone;   25
And with him are the Lord Aumerle, Lord Salisbury,
Sir Stephen Scrope, besides a clergyman
Of holy reverence; who, I cannot learn.

NORTHUMBERLAND   O, belike it is the Bishop of Carlisle.

BOLINGBROKE [*to Northumberland*]   Noble lord,   30
Go to the rude ribs of that ancient castle;
Through brazen trumpet send the breath of parley
Into his ruined ears, and thus deliver.
Henry Bolingbroke
On both his knees doth kiss King Richard's hand,   35
And sends allegiance and true faith of heart
To his most royal person, hither come
Even at his feet to lay my arms and power,
Provided that my banishment repealed
And lands restored again be freely granted.   40
If not, I'll use the advantage of my power,
And lay the summer's dust with showers of blood
Rained from the wounds of slaughtered Englishmen;
The which how far off from the mind of Bolingbroke
It is such crimson tempest should bedrench   45
The fresh green lap of fair King Richard's land
My stooping duty tenderly shall show.
Go, signify as much, while here we march
Upon the grassy carpet of this plain.
Let's march without the noise of threat'ning drum,   50
That from this castle's tottered battlements
Our fair appointments may be well perused.
Methinks King Richard and myself should meet
With no less terror than the elements
Of fire and water when their thund'ring shock   55

3.3.25 **lime** mortar
3.3.29 **belike** probably
3.3.31 **rude** rough
3.3.31 **ribs** i.e. walls
3.3.33 **ears** i.e. loop-holes
3.3.37 **come** being come (with *I*
     understood from *my*, 3.3.38)

3.3.38 **lay** make settle
3.3.44 **The which** as to which
3.3.46 **fair** (could qualify King Richard
     or land)
3.3.47 **stooping** i.e. submissive, humble
3.3.51 **tottered** tottering, tattered
3.3.52 **appointments** military preparations

At meeting tears the cloudy cheeks of heaven.
Be he the fire, I'll be the yielding water.
The rage be his, whilst on the earth I rain
My waters on the earth, and not on him.
March on, and mark King Richard how he looks.   60

[*They march about the stage, then Bolingbroke, York, Percy,
and soldiers stand at a distance from walls; Northumberland
and trumpeter advance to the walls. Parle without, and answer
within: then a flourish.*] *Richard appeareth on the walls,* [*with
the Bishop of Carlisle, the Duke of Aumerle, Scrope, Earl of
Salisbury*]

See, see. King Richard doth himself appear,
As doth the blushing discontented sun
From out the fiery portal of the east
When he perceives the envious clouds are bent
To dim his glory and to stain the track   65
Of his bright passage to the occident.

YORK   Yet looks he like a king. Behold his eye,
As bright as is the eagle's, lightens forth
Controlling majesty. Alack, alack for woe
That any harm should stain so fair a show!   70

KING RICHARD [*to Northumberland*]   We are amazed; and thus
        long have we stood
To watch the fearful bending of thy knee,
Because we thought ourself thy lawful king.
An if we be, how dare thy joints forget
To pay their aweful duty to our presence?   75
If we be not, show us the hand of God
That hath dismissed us from our stewardship.

3.3.58 **I rain** rain, rein
3.3.60.4 *on the walls* (refers to the
    upper acting area of the Elizabethan
    stage; the rear wall of the main stage
    conventionally represented castle or
    city walls)
3.3.62–6 **As…occident** i.e. the proverbial
    idea that a red sky in the morning
    anticipates bad weather
3.3.63 **From out** out of

3.3.64 **envious** malicious
3.3.64 **bent** intent
3.3.65 **stain** obscure the lustre
3.3.67 **Yet** i.e. despite the
    threatening *clouds* (or simply 'still')
3.3.68–9 **lightens…majesty** sends out
    lightning-flashes of controlling majesty
3.3.71 **We…stood** (Northumberland has
    failed to kneel to the King.)
3.3.75 **aweful** reverential

For well we know no hand of blood and bone
Can grip the sacred handle of our sceptre,
Unless he do profane, steal, or usurp.   80
And though you think that all—as you have done—
Have torn their souls by turning them from us,
And we are barren and bereft of friends,
Yet know my master, God omnipotent,
Is mustering in his clouds on our behalf   85
Armies of pestilence; and they shall strike
Your children yet unborn and unbegot,
That lift your vassal hands against my head,
And threat the glory of my precious crown.
Tell Bolingbroke, for yon methinks he stands,   90
That every stride he makes upon my land
Is dangerous treason. He is come to open
The purple testament of bleeding war;
But ere the crown he looks for live in peace,
Ten thousand bloody crowns of mothers' sons   95
Shall ill become the flower of England's face,
Change the complexion of her maid-pale peace
To scarlet indignation, and bedew
Her pastures' grass with faithful English blood.

NORTHUMBERLAND   The King of heaven forbid our lord the King   100
Should so with civil and uncivil arms
Be rushed upon. Thy thrice-noble cousin
Harry Bolingbroke doth humbly kiss thy hand,
And by the honourable tomb he swears,
That stands upon your royal grandsire's bones,   105
And by the royalties of both your bloods,
Currents that spring from one most gracious head,
And by the buried hand of warlike Gaunt,
And by the worth and honour of himself,

3.3.79 **grip** seize
3.3.83 **And** and that
3.3.88 **That** i.e. you that
3.3.92 **dangerous** i.e. threatening Richard
3.3.93 **purple** i.e. blood-coloured
3.3.93 **testament** will
3.3.95 **crowns** heads

3.3.96 **flower of England's face** flower-like face of England; the faces of the choicest youth of England
3.3.101 **civil** of the same country (as in civil war)
3.3.101 **uncivil** barbarous
3.3.107 **Currents** streams

Comprising all that may be sworn or said,   110
His coming hither hath no further scope
Than for his lineal royalties, and to beg
Enfranchisement immediate on his knees;
Which on thy royal party granted once,
His glittering arms he will commend to rust,   115
His barbèd steeds to stables, and his heart
To faithful service of your majesty.
This swears he, as he is a prince and just,
And as I am a gentleman I credit him.

KING RICHARD   Northumberland, say thus the King returns: 120
His noble cousin is right welcome hither,
And all the number of his fair demands
Shall be accomplished without contradiction.
With all the gracious utterance thou hast,
Speak to his gentle hearing kind commends.   125

   [*Northumberland and the trumpeter return to Bolingbroke*]

[*To Aumerle*] We do debase ourselves, cousin, do we not,

To look so poorly and to speak so fair?
Shall we call back Northumberland, and send
Defiance to the traitor, and so die?

AUMERLE   No, good my lord, let's fight with gentle words   130
Till time lend friends, and friends their helpful swords.

KING RICHARD   O God, O God, that e'er this tongue of mine
That laid the sentence of dread banishment
On yon proud man should take it off again
With words of sooth! O, that I were as great   135
As is my grief, or lesser than my name,
Or that I could forget what I have been,
Or not remember what I must be now!
Swell'st thou, proud heart? I'll give thee scope to beat,

3.3.111 **scope** end in view
3.3.113 **Enfranchisement** repeal
  from banishment and restitution
  of lands and rights
3.3.114 **party** part
3.3.115 **commend** commit

3.3.116 **barbèd** armed with barbs or bards
  (armoured covering for the breast and
  flanks of a horse)
3.3.119 **credit** believe
3.3.120 **returns** replies
3.3.127 **poorly** abjectly
3.3.135 **sooth** blandishment

Since foes have scope to beat both thee and me. 140

[*Northumberland advances to the wall and Richard's faction*]

AUMERLE   Northumberland comes back from Bolingbroke.

KING RICHARD   What must the King do now? Must he submit?
The King shall do it. Must he be deposed?
The King shall be contented. Must he lose
The name of King? A God's name, let it go. 145
I'll give my jewels for a set of beads,
My gorgeous palace for a hermitage,
My gay apparel for an almsman's gown,
My figured goblets for a dish of wood,
My sceptre for a palmer's walking staff, 150
My subjects for a pair of carvèd saints,
And my large kingdom for a little grave,
A little little grave, an òbscure grave;
Or I'll be buried in the King's highway,
Some way of common trade where subjects' feet 155
May hourly trample on their sovereign's head;
For on my heart they tread now whilst I live,
And, buried once, why not upon my head?
Aumerle, thou weep'st, my tender-hearted cousin.
We'll make foul weather with despisèd tears. 160
Our sighs and they shall lodge the summer corn,
And make a dearth in this revolting land.
Or shall we play the wantons with our woes,
And make some pretty match with shedding tears,
As thus to drop them still upon one place 165
Till they have fretted us a pair of graves
Within the earth, and therein laid? 'There lies
Two kinsmen digged their graves with weeping eyes.'

3.3.145 **A** in
3.3.146 **set of beads** rosary
3.3.149 **figured** engraved with patterns
3.3.150 **palmer's** pilgrim's
3.3.153 **òbscure** lowly; dark; remote
3.3.155 **trade** passage, resort
3.3.160 **despisèd** contemptible, mocked at
3.3.161 **lodge** beat down
3.3.162 **revolting** rebelling

3.3.163 **play the wantons** act playfully
3.3.164 **pretty match** clever game
3.3.165 **still** continually
3.3.166 **fretted** worn away
3.3.167 **laid** laid ourselves
3.3.167 8 **There...eyes** i.e. an 'epitaph' on the *graves*
3.3.168 **digged** i.e. who digged

Would not this ill do well? Well, well, I see
I talk but idly, and you laugh at me.   170
Most mighty prince, my lord Northumberland,
What says King Bolingbroke? Will his majesty
Give Richard leave to live till Richard die?
You make a leg, and Bolingbroke says 'Ay'.

NORTHUMBERLAND   My lord, in the base court he doth attend   175
To speak with you. May it please you to come down?

KING RICHARD   Down, down I come, like glist'ring Phaëton,
Wanting the manage of unruly jades.
In the base court: base court where kings grow base,
To come at traitors' calls, and do them grace.   180
In the base court, come down: down court, down King,
For night-owls shriek where mounting larks should sing.

                           [*Exeunt Richard and his party*]

BOLINGBROKE   What says his majesty?

NORTHUMBERLAND   Sorrow and grief of heart
Makes him speak fondly, like a frantic man.

    [*Enter King Richard and his party below*]

Yet he is come.   185

BOLINGBROKE   Stand all apart,
And show fair duty to his majesty.

    He kneels down

My gracious lord.

3.3.169 **do well** be appropriate
3.3.170 **idly** foolishly
3.3.174 **You…'Ay'** i.e. if you as a *mighty prince* petition on my behalf, Bolingbroke is bound to assent
3.3.174 **make a leg** crook the knee, make an obeisance
3.3.177 **Down, down I come** (Richard descends from the upper acting area of Elizabethan stage to main stage. In modern versions, Richard may be lowered by mechanical means or come down a visible staircase.)
3.3.177 **Phaëthon** (In Greek myth, son of the sun-god, Apollo. He rashly took his father's sun-chariot and drove it round the earth, but was too weak to control the horses. Zeus struck him down with a thunderbolt to prevent him destroying the earth.)
3.3.178 **Wanting the manage of** i.e. lacking the horsemanship to control
3.3.178 **jades** horses (a contemptuous term, here an image for Richard's noblemen)
3.3.179 **base court** outer courtyard (surrounded by stables, offices, and servants' quarters)
3.3.180 **do them grace** favour them
3.3.181 **court** courtyard; royal court
3.3.182 **night-owls** (associated with evil)
3.3.184 **fondly** foolishly, insanely
3.3.184 **frantic** insane, frenzied

KING RICHARD   Fair cousin, you debase your princely knee
　　To make the base earth proud with kissing it.
　　Me rather had my heart might feel your love   190
　　Than my unpleased eye see your courtesy.
　　Up, cousin, up. Your heart is up, I know,
　　Thus high at least, although your knee be low.

BOLINGBROKE   My gracious lord, I come but for mine own.

KING RICHARD   Your own is yours, and I am yours, and all.   195

BOLINGBROKE   So far be mine, my most redoubted lord,
　　As my true service shall deserve your love.

KING RICHARD   Well you deserve. They well deserve to have
　　That know the strong'st and surest way to get.

　　　[*Bolingbroke rises*]

　　[*To York*] Uncle, give me your hands. Nay, dry your eyes.   200

　　Tears show their love, but want their remedies.

　　[*To Bolingbroke*] Cousin, I am too young to be your father,

　　Though you are old enough to be my heir.
　　What you will have I'll give, and willing too;
　　For do we must what force will have us do.   205
　　Set on towards London, cousin: is it so?

BOLINGBROKE   Yea, my good lord.

KING RICHARD   Then I must not say no.
　　　　　　　　　　　　　　　　　　　[*Flourish. Exeunt.*]

3.4
Sc. 12   *Enter the Queen with her* [*two Ladies*]

QUEEN   What sport shall we devise here in this garden,
　　To drive away the heavy thought of care?

3.3.190 **Me rather had** i.e. I had rather
3.3.191 **courtesy** (also meaning *curtsy*, the
　　act of obeisance)
3.3.193 **Thus high** i.e. as high as my crown
3.3.196 **redoubted** dreaded
3.3.201 **want their remedies** i.e. are
　　unable to remedy their causes

Sc. 12 3.4.0 *two Ladies* (The distribution
　　of speeches between the first and second
　　Lady and the first and second Man
　　is always an editorial or performance
　　choice, the early editions identify just
　　'Lady' and 'Man'/'Servant' as the
　　speakers.)

LADY   Madam, we'll play at bowls.

QUEEN   'Twill make me think the world is full of rubs,
And that my fortune runs against the bias.   5

LADY   Madam, we'll dance.

QUEEN   My legs can keep no measure in delight
When my poor heart no measure keeps in grief;
Therefore no dancing, girl. Some other sport.

LADY   Madam, we'll tell tales.   10

QUEEN   Of sorrow or of joy?

LADY   Of either, madam.

QUEEN   Of neither, girl.
For if of joy, being altogether wanting,
It doth remember me the more of sorrow.   15
Or if of grief, being altogether had,
It adds more sorrow to my want of joy.
For what I have I need not to repeat,
And what I want it boots not to complain.

LADY   Madam, I'll sing.   20

QUEEN   'Tis well that thou hast cause;
But thou shouldst please me better wouldst thou weep.

LADY   I could weep, madam, would it do you good.

QUEEN   And I could sing, would weeping do me good,
And never borrow any tear of thee.

Enter Gardener [and two Men]

But stay, here come the gardeners.   25
Let's step into the shadow of these trees.
My wretchedness unto a row of pins

3.4.4 **rubs** obstacles, impediments (such
  as would divert a bowl from its proper
  course)
3.4.5 **bias** (the lead weight in the side of a
  bowl which makes it run in a smooth line
  or curve)
3.4.7 **can…in** cannot dance in step with
3.4.8 **no measure keeps** is boundless
3.4.15 **remember** remind

3.4.16 **had** possessed
3.4.19 **boots** helps
3.4.19 **complain** lament
3.4.22 **would…good** i.e. if only my
  sorrows were alleviated by weeping
3.4.27 **My…pins** (gambling *my
  wretchedness* as something great
  against the trivial value of *a row of pins*)

They will talk of state, for everyone doth so
Against a change. Woe is forerun with woe.

GARDENER [*to First Man*]   Go, bind thou up young dangling apricots   30
Which, like unruly children, make their sire
Stoop with oppression of their prodigal weight.
Give some supportance to the bending twigs.

[*To Second Man*] Go thou, and, like an executioner,

Cut off the heads of too-fast-growing sprays,   35
That look too lofty in our commonwealth.
All must be even in our government.
You thus employed, I will go root away
The noisome weeds which without profit suck
The soil's fertility from wholesome flowers.   40

MAN   Why should we, in the compass of a pale,
Keep law and form, and due proportïon,
Showing as in a model our firm estate,
When our sea-wallèd garden, the whole land,
Is full of weeds, her fairest flowers choked up,   45
Her fruit trees all unpruned, her hedges ruined,
Her knots disordered, and her wholesome herbs
Swarming with caterpillars?

GARDENER   Hold thy peace.
He that hath suffered this disordered spring
Hath now himself met with the fall of leaf.   50
The weeds which his broad spreading leaves did shelter,
That seemed in eating him to hold him up,
Are plucked up, root and all, by Bolingbroke—
I mean the Earl of Wiltshire, Bushy, Green.

MAN   What, are they dead?   55

GARDENER   They are. And Bolingbroke

3.4.29 **Against** in anticipation of
3.4.32 **prodigal** prodigious (of the fruit); reckless (of *unruly children*)
3.4.37 **even** equal
3.4.39 **noisome** harmful
3.4.39 **profit** i.e. benefit to the garden
3.4.41 **pale** enclosure, fence
3.4.43 **estate** government
3.4.47 **knots** intricate flowerbeds; social bonds
3.4.49 **suffered** permitted

Richard II

Hath seized the wasteful King. O, what pity is it
That he had not so trimmed and dressed his land
As we this garden! We at time of year
Do wound the bark, the skin of our fruit trees,
Lest, being over-proud in sap and blood,   60
With too much riches it confound itself.
Had he done so to great and growing men,
They might have lived to bear and he to taste
Their fruits of duty. Superfluous branches
We lop away, that bearing boughs may live.   65
Had he done so, himself had borne the crown,
Which waste of idle hours hath quite thrown down.

MAN   What, think you the King shall be deposed?

GARDENER   Depressed he is already, and deposed
'Tis doubt he will be. Letters came last night   70
To a dear friend of the good Duke of York's
That tell black tidings.

QUEEN   O, I am pressed to death through want of speaking!

[*To the Gardener*] Thou, old Adam's likeness set to dress this garden,

How dares thy harsh rude tongue sound this unpleasing news?   75
What Eve, what serpent hath suggested thee
To make a second fall of cursèd man?

3.4.56 **wasteful** desolation-causing; extravagant, spendthrift
3.4.57 **dressed** cultivated
3.4.58 **at time of year** in season
3.4.59 **wound the bark** (referring to the practice of ringing bark at blossom time, which restricts the tree's food supply and concentrates sap in the branches, so encouraging fruit buds to form)
3.4.60 **over-proud in** excessively swollen with
3.4.61 **confound** ruin
3.4.64 **Superfluous** excessive, extravagant; redundant (accented in the first and third syllables)
3.4.66 **crown** (with a quibble on the crown of a tree)
3.4.69 **Depressed** brought low

3.4.70 **doubt** feared
3.4.73 **pressed to death** (alluding to the medieval punishment of killing an accused person who maintained silence by laying ever-increasing weights on the body)
3.4.74 **dress** cultivate (The line recalls Genesis 2:15 'God took the man [Adam], and put him into the garden of Eden to dress it.')
3.4.75 **rude** ignorant
3.4.76 **suggested** tempted
3.4.77 **To…man** (emotionally implying that the Gardener's words are responsible for Richard's disposition)
3.4.77 **cursèd** (recalling God's curse on man after his first fall from grace)

Why dost thou say King Richard is deposed?
Dar'st thou, thou little better thing than earth,
Divine his downfall? Say, where, when, and how,   80
Cam'st thou by this ill tidings? Speak, thou wretch!

GARDENER   Pardon me, madam. Little joy have I
To breathe this news, yet what I say is true.
King Richard he is in the mighty hold
Of Bolingbroke. Their fortunes both are weighed.   85
In your lord's scale is nothing but himself
And some few vanities that make him light;
But in the balance of great Bolingbroke,
Besides himself, are all the English peers,
And with that odds he weighs King Richard down.   90
Post you to London and you will find it so.
I speak no more than everyone doth know.

QUEEN   Nimble mischance that art so light of foot,
Doth not thy embassage belong to me,
And am I last that knows it? O, thou think'st   95
To serve me last, that I may longest keep
Thy sorrow in my breast. Come, ladies, go
To meet at London London's king in woe.
What, was I born to this, that my sad look
Should grace the triumph of great Bolingbroke?   100
Gard'ner, for telling me these news of woe,
Pray God the plants thou graft'st may never grow.
                                              Exit [with Ladies]

GARDENER   Poor Queen, so that thy state might be no worse
I would my skill were subject to thy curse.
Here did she fall a tear. Here in this place   105
I'll set a bank of rue, sour herb of grace.
Rue even for ruth here shortly shall be seen
In the remembrance of a weeping queen.   *Exeunt.*

3.4.83 **To breathe** in speaking
3.4.85–90 **Their...down** (echoing Psalm 62:9)
3.4.87 **vanities** worthless, frivolous people
3.4.91 **Post** hasten
3.4.94 **embassage** message
3.4.103 **so that** if as a result
3.4.106 **rue** (The herb was associated with repentance on account of the abstract sense 'regret'; hence it was known as *herb of grace* (grace being the object of repentance).)
3.4.108 **In the remembrance** in memory

4.1

Sc. 13 *Enter Bolingbroke with the Lords[: the Duke of Aumerle, the
           Earl of Northumberland, Harry Percy, Lord Fitzwalter, the
           Duke of Surrey, the Bishop of Carlisle, and the Abbot of
           Westminster] to Parliament[. They sit down]*

BOLINGBROKE   Call forth Bagot.

   Enter Bagot [with officers].

   Now, Bagot, freely speak thy mind:
   What thou dost know of noble Gloucester's death,
   Who wrought it with the King, and who performed
   The bloody office of his timeless end.   5

BAGOT   Then set before my face the Lord Aumerle.

BOLINGBROKE *[to Aumerle]*   Cousin, stand forth, and look upon
       that man.

BAGOT   My lord Aumerle, I know your daring tongue
   Scorns to unsay what once it hath delivered.
   In that dead time when Gloucester's death was plotted   10
   I heard you say, 'Is not my arm of length,
   That reacheth from the restful English court,
   As far as Cálais, to mine uncle's head?
   Amongst much other talk that very time
   I heard you say that you had rather refuse   15
   The offer of an hundred thousand crowns
   Than Bolingbroke's return to England,
   Adding withal how blest this land would be
   In this your cousin's death.

AUMERLE   Princes and noble lords,
   What answer shall I make to this base man?   20
   Shall I so much dishonour my fair stars
   On equal terms to give him chastisement?
   Either I must, or have mine honour soiled

Sc. 13 4.1.4 **wrought it with** persuaded;
   or collaborated with
4.1.5 **office** duty
4.1.5 **timeless** untimely
4.1.10 **dead** fatal; dark
4.1.11 **of length** long

4.1.17 **Than** i.e. than accept
4.1.21 **fair stars** i.e. honourable birth
   (astrologically influenced)
4.1.22 **chastisement** punishment (in
   combat). A lord could refuse to fight
   a man of low birth.

With the attainder of his slanderous lips.

[*He throws down his gage*]

There is my gage, the manual seal of death,   25
That marks thee out for hell. I say thou liest,
And will maintain what thou hast said is false
In thy heart blood, though being all too base
To stain the temper of my knightly sword.

BOLINGBROKE   Bagot, forbear. Thou shalt not take it up.   30

AUMERLE   Excepting one, I would he were the best
In all this presence that hath moved me so.

FITZWALTER   If that thy valour stand on sympathy,
There is my gage, Aumerle, in gage to thine.

[*He throws down his gage*]

By that fair sun which shows me where thou stand'st,   35
I heard thee say, and vauntingly thou spak'st it,
That thou wert cause of noble Gloucester's death.
If thou deny'st it twenty times, thou liest,
And I will turn thy falsehood to thy heart,
Where it was forgèd with my rapier's point.   40

AUMERLE   Thou dar'st not, coward, live to see that day.

FITZWALTER   Now by my soul, I would it were this hour.

AUMERLE   Fitzwalter, thou art damned to hell for this.

HARRY PERCY   Aumerle, thou liest. His honour is as true
In this appeal as thou art all unjust;   45
And that thou art so, there I throw my gage

[*He throws down his gage*]

To prove it on thee to the extremest point
Of mortal breathing. Seize it if thou dar'st.

AUMERLE   An if I do not, may my hands rot off,
And never brandish more revengeful steel   50

4.1.24 **attainder** accusation
4.1.25 **manual seal** seal given with one's own hand
4.1.27 **maintain** uphold in combat
4.1.29 **temper** quality (literally 'hardness')
4.1.31 **one** i.e. Bolingbroke
4.1.31 **he** i.e. Bagot

4.1.31 **best** highest in rank
4.1.32 **moved** angered
4.1.33 **stand on sympathy** i.e. insists on equivalence of rank
4.1.38 **If** even if
4.1.45 **appeal** accusation
4.1.50 **more** again

Over the glittering helmet of my foe.

ANOTHER LORD   I task the earth to the like, forsworn Aumerle,
And spur thee on with full as many lies
As may be hollowed in thy treacherous ear
From sun to sun. There is my honour's pawn.   55
Engage it to the trial if thou darest.

AUMERLE   Who sets me else? By heaven, I'll throw at all!
I have a thousand spirits in one breast
To answer twenty thousand such as you.

SURREY   My lord Fitzwalter, I do remember well   60
The very time Aumerle and you did talk.

FITZWALTER   'Tis very true. You were in presence then,
And you can witness with me this is true.

SURREY   As false, by heaven, as heaven itself is true.

FITZWALTER   Surrey, thou liest.   65

SURREY   Dishonourable boy,
That lie shall lie so heavy on my sword
That it shall render vengeance and revenge,
Till thou, the lie-giver, and that lie do lie
In earth as quiet as thy father's skull;
In proof whereof, there is my honour's pawn.   70

    [*He throws down his gage*]

Engage it to the trial if thou dar'st.

FITZWALTER   How fondly dost thou spur a forward horse!
If I dare eat, or drink, or breathe, or live,
I dare meet Surrey in a wilderness,
And spit upon him whilst I say he lies,   75
And lies, and lies. There is my bond of faith
To tie thee to my strong correction.

4.1.53 **lies** accusations of lying
4.1.54 **hollowed** 'the thing shouted as object' *OED*; reverberated or echoed; 'hallooed'; slang for 'hollered'
4.1.55 **sun to sun** sunrise to sunset
4.1.56 **Engage it to** i.e. accept it as a pledge (*gage*) for
4.1.57 **sets** challenges (by putting down a stake, as in gambling)
4.1.57 **throw** to defeat (as by the throw of dice)
4.1.62 **in presence** present
4.1.65 **boy** (expression of contempt)
4.1.69 **quiet** silently
4.1.72 **fondly** foolishly
4.1.74 **I…wilderness** (the idea is similar to 1.1.63–5)

As I intend to thrive in this new world,
Aumerle is guilty of my true appeal.
Besides, I heard the banished Norfolk say   80
That thou, Aumerle, didst send two of thy men
To execute the noble Duke at Calais.

AUMERLE   Some honest Christian trust me with a gage.

[*He throws down another's gage*]

That Norfolk lies, here do I throw down this,
If he may be repealed, to try his honour.   85

BOLINGBROKE   These differences shall all rest under gage,
Till Norfolk be repealed. Repealed he shall be,
And, though mine enemy, restored again
To all his lands and signories. When he is returned,
Against Aumerle we will enforce his trial.   90

BISHOP OF CARLISLE   That honourable day shall never be seen.
Many a time hath banished Norfolk fought
For Jesu Christ in glorious Christian field,
Streaming the ensign of the Christian cross
Against black pagans, Turks, and Saracens;   95
And, toiled with works of war, retired himself
To Italy, and there at Venice gave
His body to that pleasant country's earth,
And his pure soul unto his captain, Christ,
Under whose colours he had fought so long.   100

BOLINGBROKE   Why, Bishop of Carlisle, is Norfolk dead?

BISHOP OF CARLISLE   As surely as I live, my lord.

BOLINGBROKE   Sweet peace conduct his sweet soul to the bosom
Of good old Abraham! Lords appellants,
Your differences shall all rest under gage   105
Till we assign you to your days of trial.

Enter York

4.1.79 **of my true appeal** as I truly
    accuse him
4.1.83 **trust me with** i.e. lend me
4.1.85 **repealed** recalled
    from exile
4.1.89 **signories** estates

4.1.93 **Christian field** battle for the
    Christian cause
4.1.96 **toiled** exhausted
4.1.103–4 **bosom…Abraham** i.e.
    heavenly rest (from Luke 16:22)
4.1.105 **differences** disputes

YORK   Great Duke of Lancaster, I come to thee
    From plume-plucked Richard, who with willing soul
    Adopts thee heir, and his high sceptre yields
    To the possession of thy royal hand.   110
    Ascend his throne, descending now from him,
    And long live Henry, fourth of that name!

BOLINGBROKE   In God's name I'll ascend the regal throne.

BISHOP OF CARLISLE   Marry, God forbid!
    Worst in this royal presence may I speak,   115
    Yet best beseeming me to speak the truth.
    Would God that any in this noble presence
    Were enough noble to be upright judge
    Of noble Richard! Then true noblesse would
    Learn him forbearance from so foul a wrong.   120
    What subject can give sentence on his king?
    And who sits here that is not Richard's subject?
    Thieves are not judged but they are by to hear,
    Although apparent guilt be seen in them;
    And shall the figure of God's majesty,   125
    His captain, steward, deputy elect,
    Anointed, crownèd, planted many years,
    Be judged by subject and inferior breath,
    And he himself not present? O, forfend it God,
    That in a Christian climate souls refined   130
    Should show so heinous, black, obscene a deed!
    I speak to subjects, and a subject speaks,
    Stirred up by God thus boldly for his king.
    My lord of Hereford here, whom you call king,

4.1.108 **plume-plucked** humbled
4.1.115 **Worst** least worthy
4.1.115 **royal presence** (probably sarcastic)
4.1.115 **may I** though I may be
4.1.116 **best beseeming me to** as it is most fitting that I should
4.1.119 **noble** (playing on the senses 'virtuous', and 'royal': a king was above the law, so could not be judged)
4.1.119 **noblesse** nobility
4.1.120 **Learn** teach
4.1.120 **him** i.e. the potential judge

4.1.123 **but** except who
4.1.123 **by** present
4.1.124 **apparent** manifest
4.1.125 **figure** image, visible representative
4.1.126 **elect** chosen
4.1.127 **planted** established
4.1.128 **subject** (an adjective)
4.1.129 **forfend** forbid
4.1.130 **climate** region
4.1.130 **refined** spiritually improved (by Christianity); having the virtue and manners of the nobility

Is a foul traitor to proud Hereford's king, 135
And if you crown him, let me prophesy
The blood of English shall manure the ground,
And future ages groan for this foul act.
Peace shall go sleep with Turks and infidels,
And in this seat of peace tumultuous wars 140
Shall kin with kin and kind with kind confound.
Disorder, horror, fear, and mutiny
Shall here inhabit, and this land be called
The field of Golgotha and dead men's skulls.
O, if you raise this house against this house, 145
It will the woefullest division prove
That ever fell upon this cursèd earth.
Prevent it, resist it, let it not be so,
Lest child, child's children, cry against you woe.

NORTHUMBERLAND   Well have you argued, sir, and for your pains 150
Of capital treason we arrest you here.
My lord of Westminster, be it your charge
To keep him safely till his day of trial.
May it please you, lords, to grant the Commons' suit?

BOLINGBROKE   Fetch hither Richard, that in common view 155
He may surrender. So we shall proceed
Without suspicion.

YORK   I will be his conduct.   *Exit*

BOLINGBROKE   Lords, you that here are under our arrest,

4.1.140 **this seat of peace** (perhaps with specific reference to the throne as source of national unity and rule of law)

4.1.141 **Shall...confound** shall destroy people fighting within the same family and the same nation

4.1.144 **Golgotha** the place of Christ's crucifixion (explained in Mark 15:22 as 'The place of a skull')

4.1.145 **this house against this house** (the two houses of Lancaster and York; the house of the nation raised against itself. The latter is suggested by Mark 3:25: 'And if a house be divided against itself, that house cannot continue'.)

4.1.147 **cursèd** i.e. by the anticipated conflicts

4.1.148 **Prevent it** (run together to give two syllables)

4.1.149 **woe** woefully (or perhaps a quoted interjection)

4.1.154 **the Commons' suit** i.e. the House of Commons' request that Richard should have judgement passed on him

4.1.154–317 **May it...fall** (This scene was added in the 1623 text.)

4.1.155–7 **Fetch...suspicion** (The legitimacy of 'the Commons' suit' depended on Richard having given up the crown.)

4.1.157 **conduct** escort

Procure your sureties for your days of answer.
Little are we beholden to your love,   160
And little looked for at your helping hands.

    Enter Richard and the Duke of York [with crown and sceptre,
    attendants]

RICHARD   Alack, why am I sent for to a king
Before I have shook off the regal thoughts
Wherewith I reigned? I hardly yet have learned
To insinuate, flatter, bow, and bend my knee.   165
Give sorrow leave a while, to tutor me
To this submission. Yet I well remember
The favours of these men. Were they not mine?
Did they not sometime cry 'All hail' to me?
So Judas did to Christ, but He in twelve   170
Found truth in all but one; I, in twelve thousand, none.
God save the King! Will no man say, 'Amen'?
Am I both priest and clerk? Well then, Amen.
God save the King, although I be not he.
And yet Amen, if heaven do think him me.   175
To do what service am I sent for hither?

YORK   To do that office of thine own good will
Which tirèd majesty did make thee offer:
The resignation of thy state and crown
To Henry Bolingbroke.   180

RICHARD   Give me the crown. [*To Bolingbroke*]   Here, cousin,
    seize the crown.
Here, cousin. On this side my hand, on that side thine.
Now is this golden crown like a deep well
That owes two buckets filling one another,
The emptier ever dancing in the air,   185

4.1.159 **sureties…answer** guarantors for
your appearance on the days of trial
4.1.160 **beholden** beholder
4.1.161 **look'd for at** is expected from
4.1.168 **favours** faces; favourable deeds
4.1.170 **So…Christ** (Judas said 'Hail
master' and kissed him in order to betray
him (Matthew 26:49).)

4.1.173 **clerk** (church officer who uttered
the responses to the prayers)
4.1.183–8 **Now…high** (a proverbial image
of the vicissitudes of fortune)
4.1.184 **owes** has
4.1.184 **filling one another** i.e. the raising
of the one causing the other to descend
and fill

The other down, unseen, and full of water.
That bucket down and full of tears am I,
Drinking my griefs, whilst you mount up on high.

BOLINGBROKE   I thought you had been willing to resign.

RICHARD   My crown I am, but still my griefs are mine.   190
You may my glories and my state depose,
But not my griefs; still am I king of those.

BOLINGBROKE   Part of your cares you give me with your crown.

RICHARD   Your cares set up do not pluck my cares down.
My care is loss of care by old care done;   195
Your care is gain of care by new care won.
The cares I give I have, though given away;
They 'tend the crown, yet still with me they stay.

BOLINGBROKE   Are you contented to resign the crown?

RICHARD   Ay, no; no, ay; for I must nothing be;   200
Therefore no, no, for I resign to thee.
Now mark me how I will undo myself.
I give this heavy weight from off my head,

[*Bolingbroke accepts the crown*]

And this unwieldy sceptre from my hand,

[*Bolingbroke accepts the sceptre*]

The pride of kingly sway from out my heart.   205
With mine own tears I wash away my balm,
With mine own hands I give away my crown,
With mine own tongue deny my sacred state,
With mine own breath release all duteous oaths.
All pomp and majesty I do forswear: 210
My manors, rents, revenues I forgo;
My acts, decrees, and statutes I deny.

4.1.191 **state** stateliness
4.1.192 **still** permanently
4.1.194–8 **Your…stay** (quibbling
on *cares* as 'responsibilities', 'griefs',
'diligence', and 'anxiety' in turn)
4.1.195 **by old care done** brought about
by my diligence (i.e. lack of it) in
times past

4.1.200 **Ay…be** (quibbling on 'by' and
'I'; 'nothing' could be pronounced
'no thing')
4.1.202 **undo** ruin; divest, strip
4.1.209 **duteous oaths** oaths of allegiance
4.1.211 **revenues** (accented on the second
syllable)
4.1.212 **deny** repudiate

God pardon all oaths that are broke to me.
God keep all vows unbroke are made to thee.
Make me, that nothing have, with nothing grieved,   215
And thou with all pleased, that hast all achieved.
Long mayst thou live in Richard's seat to sit,
And soon lie *Richard* in an earthy pit.
'God save King *Henry*,' unkinged *Richard* says,
'And send him many years of sunshine days.'   220
What more remains?

NORTHUMBERLAND [*giving Richard papers*]   No more but that
    you read
These accusations and these grievous crimes
Committed by your person and your followers
Against the state and profit of this land,
That by confessing them, the souls of men   225
May deem that you are worthily deposed.

RICHARD   Must I do so? And must I ravel out
My weaved-up follies? Gentle *Northumberland*,
If thy offences were upon record,
Would it not shame thee, in so fair a troop,   230
To read a lecture of them? If thou wouldst,
There shouldst thou find one heinous article
Containing the deposing of a king
And cracking the strong warrant of an oath,
Marked with a blot, damned in the book of heaven.   235
Nay, all of you that stand and look upon me
Whilst that my wretchedness doth bait myself,
Though some of you, with Pilate, wash your hands,
Showing an outward pity, yet you Pilates
Have here delivered me to my sour cross,   240
And water cannot wash away your sin.

NORTHUMBERLAND   My lord, dispatch. Read o'er these articles.

RICHARD   Mine eyes are full of tears; I cannot see.

4.1.215 **Make** i.e. God make
4.1.224 **state** settled order
4.1.229 **record** (accented on the second
  syllable)

4.1.231 **read a lecture** give a public reading
4.1.234 **an oath** (probably the oath of
  allegiance)
4.1.240 **sour** bitter; sad

And yet salt water blinds them not so much
But they can see a sort of traitors here.   245
Nay, if I turn mine eyes upon myself
I find myself a traitor with the rest,
For I have given here my soul's consent
T'undeck the pompous body of a king,
Made glory base and sovereignty a slave,   250
Proud majesty a subject, state a peasant.

NORTHUMBERLAND   My lord—

RICHARD   No lord of thine, thou haught insulting man,
Nor no man's lord. I have no name, no title,
No, not that name was given me at the font,   255
But 'tis usurped. Alack the heavy day
That I have worn so many winters out
And know not now what name to call myself!
O, that I were a mockery king of snow,
Standing before the sun of Bolingbroke   260
To melt myself away in water drops!
Good King, great King—and yet not greatly good—
And if my word be sterling yet in England,
Let it command a mirror hither straight,
That it may show me what a face I have,   265
Since it is bankrupt of his majesty.

BOLINGBROKE   Go some of you and fetch a looking-glass.
                                        [*Exit one*]

NORTHUMBERLAND [*to Richard*]   Read o'er this paper while the
     glass doth come.

RICHARD   Fiend, thou torment'st me ere I come to hell.

BOLINGBROKE   Urge it no more, my lord Northumberland.   270

NORTHUMBERLAND   The Commons will not then be satisfied.

RICHARD   They shall be satisfied: I'll read enough
     When I do see the very book indeed
     Where all my sins are writ, and that's myself.

     Enter one with a glass

4.1.245 **sort** band, pack
4.1.253 **haught** haughty
4.1.266 **bankrupt** stripped bare
4.1.266 **his** its
4.1.267 **some of you** someone
4.1.268 **while** till

Give me that glass, and therein will I read.   275

    [*Richard takes the glass and looks in it*]

No deeper wrinkles yet? Hath sorrow struck
So many blows upon this face of mine
And made no deeper wounds? O flatt'ring glass,
Like to my followers in prosperity,
Thou dost beguile me. Was this face the face   280
That every day under his household roof
Did keep ten thousand men? Was this the face
That like the sun did make beholders wink?
Is this the face which faced so many follies,
That was at last outfaced by Bolingbroke?   285
A brittle glory shineth in this face.
As brittle as the glory is the face,

    He shatters the glass

For there it is, cracked in an hundred shivers.
Mark, silent King, the moral of this sport:
How soon my sorrow hath destroyed my face.   290

BOLINGBROKE   The shadow of your sorrow hath destroyed
The shadow of your face.

RICHARD   Say that again:
'The shadow of my sorrow'—ha, let's see.
'Tis very true: my grief lies all within,
And these external manner of laments   295
Are merely shadows to the unseen grief
That swells with silence in the tortured soul.
There lies the substance, and I thank thee, King,
For thy great bounty that not only giv'st
Me cause to wail, but teachest me the way   300
How to lament the cause. I'll beg one boon,
And then be gone, and trouble you no more.
Shall I obtain it?

BOLINGBROKE   Name it, fair cousin.

4.1.279 **my...prosperity** those who
  followed me when I was prosperous
4.1.284 **faced** countenanced; covered,
  adorned (as of a garment covered with
  new cloth)

4.1.288 **shivers** splinters
4.1.291 **shadow** outward show;
  or darkness
4.1.292 **shadow** image
4.1.296 **to** as

RICHARD   Fair cousin? I am greater than a king;
For when I was a king, my flatterers   305
Were then but subjects; being now a subject,
I have a king here to my flatterer.
Being so great, I have no need to beg.

BOLINGBROKE   Yet ask.

RICHARD   And shall I have?   310

BOLINGBROKE   You shall.

RICHARD   Then give me leave to go.

BOLINGBROKE   Whither?

RICHARD   Whither you will, so I were from your sights.

BOLINGBROKE   Go some of you, convey him to the Tower.   315

RICHARD   O good—'convey'. Conveyers are you all,
That rise thus nimbly by a true king's fall.   [*Exit, guarded*]

BOLINGBROKE   On Wednesday next, we solemnly set down
Our coronation. Lords, prepare yourselves.
Exeunt. Abbot of Westminster, the Bishop of Carlisle, Aumerle stay

ABBOT OF WESTMINSTER   A woeful pageant have we here beheld.   320

BISHOP OF CARLISLE   The woe's to come, the children yet unborn
Shall feel this day as sharp to them as thorn.

AUMERLE   You holy clergymen, is there no plot
To rid the realm of this pernicious blot?

ABBOT OF WESTMINSTER   My lord, before I freely speak my   325
    mind herein,
You shall not only take the sacrament
To bury mine intents, but also to effect
Whatever I shall happen to devise.
I see your brows are full of discontent,
Your hearts of sorrow, and your eyes of tears: 330
Come home with me to supper. I will lay
A plot shall show us all a merry day.   *Exeunt.*

4.1.308 **so** provided that
4.1.315 **convey** conduct,
    escort
4.1.316 **Conveyers** escorts; thieves,
    underhand contrives; transferers of
    property, merchants

4.1.322 **Shall** who shall
4.1.326 **take the sacrament** made
    a solemn oath (perhaps with an
    accompanying rite)
4.1.327 **bury mine intents** keep my
    intentions secret

5.1

Sc. 14   *Enter the Queen with her [Ladies]*

QUEEN   This way the King will come. This is the way
  To Julius Caesar's ill-erected Tower,
  To whose flint bosom my condemnèd lord
  Is doomed a prisoner by proud Bolingbroke.
  Here let us rest, if this rebellious earth   5
  Have any resting for her true king's queen.

     Enter Richard [and guard]

  But soft, but see—or, rather do not see—
  My fair rose wither. Yet look up, behold,
  That you in pity may dissolve to dew,
  And wash him fresh again with true-love tears.   10
  Ah, thou the model where old Troy did stand!
  Thou map of honour, thou King Richard's tomb,
  And not King Richard! Thou most beauteous inn,
  Why should hard-favoured grief be lodged in thee
  When triumph is become an alehouse guest?   15

RICHARD   Join not with grief, fair woman, do not so,
  To make my end too sudden. Learn, good soul,
  To think our former state a happy dream,
  From which awaked, the truth of what we are
  Shows us but this. I am sworn brother, sweet,   20
  To grim necessity, and he and I
  Will keep a league till death. Hie thee to France,
  And cloister thee in some religious house.
  Our holy lives must win a new world's crown,
  Which our profane hours here have thrown down.   25

QUEEN   What, is my Richard both in shape and mind
  Transformed and weakened? Hath Bolingbroke

Sc. 14   5.1.2 **Julius ... Tower** i.e. the Tower
  of London (wrongly thought to have been
  built by Caesar)
5.1.2 **ill-erected** erected with evil results
5.1.3 **flint** hard; of flint-bearing rock
5.1.7 **soft** wait
5.1.11 **model ... stand** i.e. representation
  of Troy's ruined greatness
5.1.12 **map** epitome

5.1.12–13 **King ... Richard** i.e. memorial
  of Richard's greatness, but not that
  greatness itself
5.1.14 **hard-favoured** ugly; ill-fortuned
5.1.15 **alehouse** (a lower class of lodging
  than an inn; the alehouse is
  Bolingbroke)
5.1.23 **religious house** convent
5.1.24 **a new world's** i.e. heaven's

Deposed thine intellect? Hath he been in thy heart?
The lion dying thrusteth forth his paw
And wounds the earth, if nothing else, with rage   30
To be o'er-powered; and wilt thou, pupil-like,
Take the correction, mildly kiss the rod,
And fawn on rage with base humility,
Which art a lion and the king of beasts?

RICHARD   A king of beasts indeed! If aught but beasts,   35
I had been still a happy king of men.
Good sometimes Queen, prepare thee hence for France.
Think I am dead, and that even here thou tak'st,
As from my deathbed, thy last living leave.
In winter's tedious nights, sit by the fire   40
With good old folks and let them tell thee tales
Of woeful ages long ago betid;
And ere thou bid goodnight, to quit their griefs
Tell thou the lamentable tale of me,
And send the hearers weeping to their beds;   45
For why the senseless brands will sympathize
The heavy accent of thy moving tongue,
And in compassion weep the fire out;
And some will mourn in ashes, some coal black,
For the deposing of a rightful king.   50

Enter Northumberland

NORTHUMBERLAND   My lord, the mind of Bolingbroke is changed.
You must to Pomfret, not unto the Tower.
And, madam, there is order ta'en for you:

5.1.31 **To be** at being
5.1.32 **kiss the rod** (proverbial)
5.1.34 **Which** i.e. 'thou'
5.1.37 **sometimes** former
5.1.42 **betid** happened
5.1.43 **quit** repay
5.1.43 **griefs** recitals of grief
5.1.44 **lamentable** (accented on the first and third syllables)
5.1.44 **tale of me** (the 'fall of princes' was a common type of narrative)
5.1.46 **For why** i.e. an account of which tale

5.1.46 **senseless** insentient
5.1.46 **sympathize** respond in empathy with
5.1.47 **heavy accent** sorrowful utterance
5.1.47 **moving** (in both literal and figurative senses)
5.1.49 **some** i.e. some of the brands
5.1.49 **ashes** (alluding to the biblical token of mourning)
5.1.52 **Pomfret** i.e. Pontefract, a town and castle in West Yorkshire
5.1.53 **there is order ta'en** arrangements have been made

With all swift speed you must away to France.

RICHARD   Northumberland, thou ladder wherewithal   55
The mounting Bolingbroke ascends my throne,
The time shall not be many hours of age
More than it is ere foul sin, gathering head,
Shall break into corruption. Thou shalt think,
Though he divide the realm and give thee half,   60
It is too little, helping him to all.
He shall think that thou, which know'st the way
To plant unrightful kings, wilt know again,
Being ne'er so little urged another way,
To pluck him headlong from the usurpèd throne.   65
The love of wicked men converts to fear,
That fear to hate, and hate turns one or both
To worthy danger and deservèd death.

NORTHUMBERLAND   My guilt be on my head, and there an end.
Take leave and part, for you must part forthwith.   70

RICHARD   Doubly divorced! Bad men, you violate
A two-fold marriage: 'twixt my crown and me,
And then betwixt me and my married wife.
[*To the Queen*] Let me unkiss the oath 'twixt thee and me—
And yet not so, for with a kiss 'twas made.   75
Part us, Northumberland: I towards the north,
Where shivering cold and sickness pines the clime;
My wife to France, from whence set forth in pomp
She came adornèd hither like sweet May,
Sent back like Hallowmas or short'st of day.   80

QUEEN   And must we be divided? Must we part?

RICHARD   Ay, hand from hand, my love, and heart from heart.

5.1.58 **foul…head** (the image is of a
 gathering boil)
5.1.59 **corruption** (specifically 'pus')
5.1.61 **helping** as you helped
5.1.66 **The…men** wicked men's love; love
 for wicked men
5.1.68 **worthy** well-deserved
5.1.70 **part…part** bid farewell…depart
5.1.77 **pines the clime** afflicts the region

5.1.78 **wife** (The 1623 text prints
 'queen' (emphasizing royalty) for
 'wife' (emphasizing their personal
 relationship), a variant with implications
 for different ways of playing the
 relationship between the Queen and
 Richard here.)
5.1.80 **Hallowmas** i.e. 1 November
5.1.80 **short'st of** the shortest

QUEEN [*to Northumberland*]   Banish us both, and send the King
    with me.

NORTHUMBERLAND   That were some love, but little policy.

QUEEN   Then whither he goes, thither let me go.   85

RICHARD   So two together weeping make one woe.
    Weep thou for me in France, I for thee here.
    Better far off than, near, be ne'er the nea'er.
    Go count thy way with sighs, I mine with groans.

QUEEN   So longest way shall have the longest moans.   90

RICHARD   Twice for one step I'll groan, the way being short,
    And piece the way out with a heavy heart.
    Come, come, in wooing sorrow let's be brief,
    Since, wedding it, there is such length in grief.
    One kiss shall stop our mouths, and dumbly part.   95
    Thus give I mine, and thus take I thy heart.

    [*They kiss*]

QUEEN   Give me mine own again. 'Twere no good part
    To take on me to keep and kill thy heart.

    [*They kiss again*]

    So now I have mine own again, be gone,
    That I may strive to kill it with a groan   100

RICHARD   We make woe wanton with this fond delay.
    Once more, adieu. The rest let sorrow say.
                      Exeunt in different directions

5.2
Sc. 15   *Enter the Duke of York and the Duchess of York*

DUCHESS OF YORK   My lord, you told me you would tell the rest,
    When weeping made you break the story off,
    Of our two cousins' coming into London.

5.1.84 **little policy** politically naive
5.1.86 **So…woe** (objecting that this would
  be a waste of tears)
5.1.88 **near…nea'er** being near, but no
  nearer our happiness
5.1.90 **So** thereby

5.1.92 **piece the way out** lengthen the way
5.1.95 **dumbly part** make us separate in
  silence
5.1.96 **mine** i.e. my heart
5.1.98 **kill** (with grief)
5.1.101 **wanton** unrestrained; flirtatious

YORK   Where did I leave?

DUCHESS OF YORK   At that sad stop, my lord,
  Where rude misgoverned hands from windows' tops.   5
  Threw dust and rubbish on King Richard's head.

YORK   Then, as I said, the Duke, great Bolingbroke,
  Mounted upon a hot and fiery steed,
  Which his aspiring rider seemed to know,
  With slow but stately pace kept on his course,   10
  Whilst all tongues cried, 'God save thee, Bolingbroke!'
  You would have thought the very windows spoke,
  So many greedy looks of young and old
  Through casements darted their desiring eyes
  Upon his visage, and that all the walls   15
  With painted imagery had said at once,
  'Jesu preserve thee, welcome Bolingbroke!'
  Whilst he, from the one side to the other turning,
  Bare-headed, lower than his proud steed's neck,
  Bespoke them thus: 'I thank you countrymen',   20
  And thus still doing, thus he passed along.

DUCHESS OF YORK   Alack, poor Richard! Where rode he the whilst?

YORK   As in a theatre the eyes of men,
  After a well-graced actor leaves the stage,
  Are idly bent on him that enters next,   25
  Thinking his prattle to be tedious,
  Even so, or with much more contempt, men's eyes
  Did scowl on gentle Richard. No man cried 'God save him!'
  No joyful tongue gave him his welcome home;
  But dust was thrown upon his sacred head,   30
  Which with such gentle sorrow he shook off,
  His face still combating with tears and smiles,
  The badges of his grief and patience,

Sc. 15 5.2.5 **rude** ignorant; brutal
5.2.5 **misgoverned** unruly
5.2.5 **windows' tops** upper-storey windows
5.2.9 **Which** (the subject of 'seemed to know')
5.2.16 **painted imagery** i.e. painted cloths, such as were hung on the walls in pageants; figures in some of these had gratulatory 'speech bubbles'
5.2.32 **combating with** expressing the combat between
5.2.33 **badges** heraldic emblems

That had not God for some strong purpose steeled
The hearts of men, they must perforce have melted,   35
And barbarism itself have pitied him.
But heaven hath a hand in these events,
To whose high will we bound our calm contents.
To Bolingbroke are we sworn subjects now,
Whose state and honour I for ay allow.   40

    [*Enter the Duke of Aumerle*]

DUCHESS OF YORK   Here comes my son Aumerle.

YORK   Aumerle that was;
But that is lost for being Richard's friend,
And, madam, you must call him 'Rutland' now.
I am in Parliament pledge for his truth
And lasting fealty to the new-made King.   45

DUCHESS OF YORK   Welcome, my son. Who are the violets now
That strew the green lap of the new-come spring?

AUMERLE   Madam, I know not, nor I greatly care not.
God knows I had as lief be none as one.

YORK   Well, bear you well in this new spring of time,   50
Lest you be cropped before you come to prime.
What news from Oxford? Do these jousts and triumphs hold?

AUMERLE   For aught I know, my lord, they do.

YORK   You will be there, I know.

AUMERLE   If God prevent it not, I purpose so.   55

YORK   What seal is that that hangs without thy bosom?
Yea, look'st thou pale? Let me see the writing.

AUMERLE   My lord, 'tis nothing.

YORK   No matter then who see it.
I will be satisfied. Let me see the writing.

5.2.40 **ay** ever. Also, a pun on 'I', 'ay', and 'eye'.
5.2.41 **Aumerle that was** (Aumerle has been deprived of his title following the dispute in 4.1.)
5.2.44 **pledge for his truth** guarantor of his loyalty

5.2.45 **fealty** fidelity (to a feudal overlord)
5.2.52 **Do** will
5.2.52 **triumphs** processional shows
5.2.52 **hold** are (they) to be held
5.2.55 **purpose** intend
5.2.56 **hangs without** protrudes from
5.2.59 **satisfied** fully answered

AUMERLE   I do beseech your grace to pardon me.   60
  It is a matter of small consequence,
  Which for some reasons I would not have seen.

YORK   Which for some reasons, sir, I mean to see.
  I fear, I fear—

DUCHESS OF YORK   What should you fear?
  'Tis nothing but some bond that he is entered into   65
  For gay apparel 'gainst the triumph day.

YORK   Bound to himself? What doth he with a bond
  That he is bound to? Wife, thou art a fool.
  Boy, let me see the writing.

AUMERLE   I do beseech you pardon me. I may not show it.   70

YORK   I will be satisfied. Let me see it, I say.

  He plucks it out of his bosom and reads it

Treason, foul treason! Villain, traitor, slave!

DUCHESS OF YORK   What is the matter, my lord?

YORK [*calls offstage*]   Ho, who is within there?

  [*Enter Servingman*]

                                        Saddle my horse.
  God for His mercy, what treachery is here!   75

DUCHESS OF YORK   Why, what is it, my lord?

YORK   Give me my boots, I say. Saddle my horse.

                                  [*Exit Servingman*]
  Now by mine honour, by my life, my troth
  I will appeach the villain.

DUCHESS OF YORK   What is the matter?   80

YORK   Peace, foolish woman.

DUCHESS OF YORK   I will not peace. What is the matter, Aumerle?

AUMERLE   Good mother, be content. It is no more
  Than my poor life must answer.

DUCHESS OF YORK   Thy life answer?

5.2.60 **pardon** excuse
5.2.66 **'gainst** in time for
5.2.67 **Bound to himself?** (The bond documenting a loan would be kept by the lender.)

5.2.79 **appeach** inform against
5.2.82 **Aumerle** (The 1623 text prints 'son' (emphasizing personal relationships) for the more formal 'Aumerle'.)

140

YORK   Bring me my boots. I will unto the King.   85

His man enters with his boots

DUCHESS OF YORK   Strike him, Aumerle! Poor boy, thou art amazed.
[*To Servingman*] Hence, villain! Never more come in my sight.

YORK [*to Servingman*]   Give me my boots, I say.

DUCHESS OF YORK   Why, York, what wilt thou do?
Wilt thou not hide the trespass of thine own?
Have we more sons? Or are we like to have?   90
Is not my teeming date drunk up with time?
And wilt thou pluck my fair son from mine age,
And rob me of a happy mother's name?
Is he not like thee? Is he not thine own?

YORK   Thou fond, mad woman,   95
Wilt thou conceal this dark conspiracy?
A dozen of them here have ta'en the sacrament,
And interchangeably set down their hands
To kill the King at Oxford.

DUCHESS OF YORK   He shall be none.
We'll keep him here; then what is that to him?   100

YORK   Away, fond woman! Were he twenty times my son,
I would appeach him.

DUCHESS OF YORK   Hadst thou groaned for him
As I have done, thou wouldst be more pitiful.
But now I know thy mind: thou dost suspect
That I have been disloyal to thy bed,   105
And that he is a bastard, not thy son.
Sweet York, sweet husband, be not of that mind.
He is as like thee as a man may be,
Not like to me, or any of my kin,

5.2.86 **him** i.e. the servant
5.2.86 **amazed** distraught
5.2.91 **teeming date** period of childbearing
5.2.91 **drunk up** i.e. made dry and infertile
5.2.91 **with** by
5.2.95 **fond** foolish

5.2.98 **interchangeably** reciprocally
5.2.98 **set down their hands** committed themselves in writing
5.2.99 **be none** not be one of them
5.2.100 **that** i.e. the bond
5.2.102 **groaned** suffered labour-pains

And yet I love him.   110

YORK   Make way, unruly woman.

                       Exit [*with Servingman*]

DUCHESS OF YORK   After, Aumerle! Mount thee upon his horse.
   Spur, post, and get before him to the King,
   And beg thy pardon ere he do accuse thee.
   I'll not be long behind—though I be old,
   I doubt not but to ride as fast as York—   115
   And never will I rise up from the ground
   Till Bolingbroke have pardoned thee. Away, be gone!

                      [*Exeunt severally*]

5.3

Sc. 16   *Enter* [*Bolingbroke, now*] *the King*], *with his nobles,* [*among
     them Harry Percy*]

KING HENRY   Can no man tell of my unthrifty son?
   'Tis full three months since I did see him last.
   If any plague hang over us, 'tis he.
   I would to God, my lords, he might be found.
   Enquire at London, 'mongst the taverns there,   5
   For there, they say, he daily doth frequent
   With unrestrainèd loose companïons,
   Even such, they say, as stand in narrow lanes
   And beat our watch and rob our passengers,
   Which he, young wanton and effeminate boy,   10
   Takes on the point of honour to support
   So dissolute a crew.

HARRY PERCY   My lord, some two days since I saw the Prince,
   And told him of those triumphs held at Oxford.

5.2.110.1 *with Servingman* See note
   to 5.2.86.
5.2.112 **post** ride fast

Sc. 16 5.3.1 **unthrifty** unrestrained,
dissolute, wasteful. The dissolute
lifestyle of this son, Prince Hal (later
Henry V), is the subject of the next two
plays in the cycle, *1, 2 Henry IV*.
5.3.3 **plague** (implying 'divine punishment')

5.3.9 **watch** watchmen
5.3.9 **passengers** wayfarers
5.3.10 **wanton** (may be adjective
   or noun)
5.3.10 **effeminate** self-indulgent,
   pleasure-seeking
5.3.11 **Takes** undertakes (also 'seizes')
5.3.11 **on the** as a
5.3.12 **dissolute** lawless (as well as modern
   senses)

KING HENRY   And what said the gallant?   15

HARRY PERCY   His answer was he would unto the stews,
And from the common'st creature pluck a glove,
And wear it as a favour, and with that,
He would unhorse the lustiest challenger.

KING HENRY   As dissolute as desperate. Yet through both   20
I see some sparks of better hope, which elder years
May happily bring forth.

Enter the Duke of Aumerle, amazed

But who comes here?

AUMERLE   Where is the King?

KING HENRY   What means our cousin that he stares and looks
so wildly?

AUMERLE   God save your grace! I do beseech your majesty   25
To have some conference with your grace alone.

KING HENRY [*to lords*]   Withdraw yourselves, and leave us here
alone.   [*Exeunt all but King Henry and Aumerle*]
What is the matter with our cousin now?

AUMERLE   For ever may my knees grow to the earth,
My tongue cleave to the roof within my mouth,   30
Unless a pardon ere I rise or speak.

KING HENRY   Intended or committed was this fault?
If on the first, how heinous e'er it be,
To win thy after-love, I pardon thee.

AUMERLE   Then give me leave that I may turn the key,   35
That no man enter till my tale be done.

5.3.16 **stews** brothels
5.3.17 **common'st** most inferior, vulgar; most indiscriminately used
5.3.17 **pluck a glove** (with a possible sexual innuendo)
5.3.18 **favour** i.e. lady's gift to a knight worn in combat as a mark of her favour; sexual favour
5.3.18 **with** i.e. wearing
5.3.19 **unhorse** (another possible innuendo: to 'horse' could be to 'cover a mare' in the sexual sense)

5.3.19 **lustiest** most vigorous (and 'most lustful')
5.3.20 **desperate** reckless
5.3.22 **happily** happily; perhaps
5.3.22.1 *amazed* distraught
5.3.29 **grow** become fixed
5.3.30 **My...mouth** (from Psalm 137:6 'let my tongue cleave to the roof of my mouth')
5.3.30 **cleave** adhere

KING HENRY   Have thy desire.

[*Aumerle locks the door.*] *The Duke of York knocks at the door and crieth*

YORK [*within*]   My liege beware, look to thyself!
Thou hast a traitor in thy presence there.

KING HENRY [*to Aumerle*]   Villain, I'll make thee safe.   40

[*King Henry begins to draw his sword*]

AUMERLE   Stay thy revengeful hand! Thou hast no cause to fear.

YORK   Open the door, secure foolhardy King!
Shall I for love speak treason to thy face?
Open the door, or I will break it open!

[*King Henry opens the door. Enter York*]

KING HENRY   What is the matter, uncle? Speak,   45
Recover breath, tell us how near is danger,
That we may arm us to encounter it.

YORK   Peruse this writing here, and thou shalt know
The treason that my haste forbids me show.

[*York presents the paper to King Henry*]

AUMERLE   Remember, as thou read'st, thy promise past.   50
I do repent me. Read not my name there;
My heart is not confederate with my hand.

YORK   It was, villain, ere thy hand did set it down.
I tore it from the traitor's bosom, King.
Fear, and not love, begets his penitence.   55
Forget to pity him, lest pity prove
A serpent that will sting thee to the heart.

KING HENRY   O, heinous, strong, and bold conspiracy!
O loyal father of a treacherous son!

5.3.40 **make thee safe** render you harmless
5.3.41 **Stay** restrain
5.3.42 **secure** overconfident
5.3.43 **for** out of
5.3.43 **treason** i.e. treasonable criticism, as in 5.3.42
5.3.49 **my haste** (York is out of breath)

5.3.49 **show** explain, tell
5.3.52 **hand** signature; hand (that wrote). York's reply takes up the latter, but *set it down* returns to 'signature'.
5.3.53 **It was** (pronounced as one syllable)
5.3.54 **it** i.e. the bond
5.3.56 **to** how to
5.3.58 **strong** gross

Thou sheer, immaculate, and silver fountain,   60
From whence this stream through muddy passages
Hath held his current and defiled himself,
Thy overflow of good converts to bad,
And thy abundant goodness shall excuse
This deadly blot in thy digressing son.   65

YORK   So shall my virtue be his vice's bawd,
And he shall spend mine honour with his shame,
As thriftless sons their scraping fathers' gold.
Mine honour lives when his dishonour dies,
Or my shamed life in his dishonour lies.   70
Thou kill'st me in his life: giving him breath
The traitor lives, the true man's put to death.

DUCHESS OF YORK [*within*]   What ho, my liege, for God's sake let
    me in!

KING HENRY   What shrill-voiced suppliant makes this eager cry?

DUCHESS OF YORK [*within*]   A woman, and thy aunt, great King;   75
    'tis I.
Speak with me, pity me, open the door!
A beggar begs that never begged before.

KING HENRY   Our scene is altered from a serious thing,
And now changed to 'The Beggar and the King'.
My dangerous cousin, let your mother in.   80
I know she is come to pray for your foul sin.

    [*Aumerle opens the door. Enter Duchess of York*]

YORK   If thou do pardon, whosoever pray,
More sins for this forgiveness prosper may.
This festered joint cut off, the rest rest sound.
This let alone will all the rest confound.   85

    [*Duchess kneels*]

5.3.60 **sheer** clear, pure
5.3.60 **fountain** spring
5.3.61 **this stream** i.e. Aumerle
5.3.64 **abundant** overflowing
5.3.65 **deadly** damnable; death-causing
5.3.65 **digressing** transgressing; diverging from the right course (as of a stream)
5.3.70 **my…lies** my life lies shamed in his dishonour
5.3.74 **eager** ardent, impetuous
5.3.79 **The…King** (the name of a ballad)
5.3.84 **festered joint** festering limb
5.3.84 **cut off** being cut off (i.e. 'cut from the body', but also executed)
5.3.85 **confound** destroy, overthrow

DUCHESS OF YORK   O King, believe not this hard-hearted man.
    Love loving not itself, none other can.

YORK   Thou frantic woman, what dost thou make here?
    Shall thy old dugs once more a traitor rear?

DUCHESS OF YORK   Sweet York, be patient. [*To King Henry*] Hear   90
    me, gentle liege.

KING HENRY   Rise up, good aunt.

DUCHESS OF YORK   Not yet, I thee beseech.
    For ever will I walk upon my knees,
    And never see day that the happy sees,
    Till thou give joy, until thou bid me joy,
    By pardoning Rutland my transgressing boy.   95

      [*Aumerle kneels*]

AUMERLE   Unto my mother's prayers I bend my knee.

      [*York kneels*]

YORK   Against them both my true joints bended be,
    Ill mayst thou thrive if thou grant any grace.

DUCHESS OF YORK   Pleads he in earnest? Look upon his face.
    His eyes do drop no tears, his prayers are in jest;   100
    His words come from his mouth, ours from our breast.
    He prays but faintly, and would be denied;
    We pray with heart and soul, and all beside.
    His weary joints would gladly rise, I know;
    Our knees shall kneel till to the ground they grow.   105
    His prayers are full of false hypocrisy;
    Ours of true zeal and deep integrity.
    Our prayers do outpray his; then let them have
    That mercy which true prayer ought to have.

KING HENRY   Good aunt, stand up.   110

DUCHESS OF YORK   Nay, do not say 'Stand up'.
    Say 'Pardon' first, and afterwards 'Stand up'.
    An if I were thy nurse, thy tongue to teach,
    'Pardon' should be the first word of thy speech.

5.3.87 **Love…itself** i.e. if one cannot love   5.3.94 **bid me joy** bid me be joyful
  one's own flesh and blood   5.3.96 **Unto** in support of
5.3.88 **make** do

I never longed to hear a word till now.
Say 'Pardon', King; let pity teach thee how.   115
The word is short, but not so short as sweet;
No word like 'Pardon' for kings' mouths so meet.

YORK   Speak it in French, King: say, 'Pardonnez-moi'.

DUCHESS OF YORK [*to York*]   Dost thou teach pardon pardon to
    destroy?
Ah, my sour husband, my hard-hearted lord,   120
That sets the word itself against the word.
[*To King Henry*] Speak 'Pardon' as 'tis current in our land;
The chopping French we do not understand.
Thine eye begins to speak; set thy tongue there;
Or in thy piteous heart plant thou thine ear,   125
That hearing how our plaints and prayers do pierce,
Pity may move thee 'Pardon' to rehearse.

KING HENRY   Good aunt, stand up.

DUCHESS OF YORK   I do not sue to stand.
Pardon is all the suit I have in hand.

KING HENRY   I pardon him as God shall pardon me.   130

    [*York and Aumerle rise*]

DUCHESS OF YORK   O, happy vantage of a kneeling knee!
Yet am I sick for fear; speak it again.
Twice saying 'Pardon' doth not pardon twain,
But makes one pardon strong.

KING HENRY   With all my heart
I pardon him.   135

    [*Duchess rises*]

DUCHESS OF YORK   A god on earth thou art.

5.3.116 **short as sweet** (suggesting the
  saying *short and sweet*)
5.3.117 **meet** fit
5.3.118 **Pardonnez-moi** French for
  'excuse me'; a polite way of saying 'no'.
5.3.118 **moi** (rhymes with 'destroy')
5.3.120 **sour** harsh
5.3.123 **chopping** jerky, abrupt;
  hair-splitting; bandying,

argumentative (perhaps also 'altering,
  changing')
5.3.124 **speak** i.e. express itself through
  weeping
5.3.126 **plaints** lamentations
5.3.127 **rehearse** recite (rhymes with *pierce*)
5.3.131 **vantage** advantage, superior
  position
5.3.133 **twain** divide

KING HENRY   But for our trusty brother-in-law and the Abbot,
    With all the rest of that consorted crew,
    Destruction straight shall dog them at the heels.
    Good uncle, help to order several powers
    To Oxford, or where'er these traitors are.   140
    They shall not live within this world, I swear,
    But I will have them if I once know where.
    Uncle, farewell; and cousin, so adieu.
    Your mother well hath prayed, and prove you true.
DUCHESS OF YORK   Come, my old son. I pray God make thee   145
    new.
       Exeunt [*King Henry at one door, York and family at the other*]

5.4
Sc. 17   [*Enter Sir Piers Exton and his Men*]

EXTON   Didst thou not mark the King, what words he spoke?
    'Have I no friend will rid me of this living fear?'
    Was it not so?
MAN   These were his very words.
EXTON   'Have I no friend?' quoth he. He spoke it twice,
    And urged it twice together, did he not?   5
MAN   He did.
EXTON   And speaking it, he wishtly looked on me,
    As who should say, 'I would thou wert the man
    That would divorce this terror from my heart',
    Meaning the King at Pomfret. Come, let's go.   10
    I am the King's friend, and will rid his foe.   *Exeunt*

5.3.136 **our trusty brother-in-law** i.e.
  the Duke of Exeter; only elsewhere
  mentioned at 2.1.282
5.3.137 **consorted** confederated (expresses
  contempt)
5.3.139 **order several powers** direct
  various forces
5.3.144 **true** loyal
5.3.145 **Come...new** (recalls the Baptism
  Service: 'O merciful God, grant that

the old Adam in this child may be
so buried that the new man may be
raised up in him')

Sc. 17 5.4.5 **together** running
5.4.7 **wishtly** intently;
  longingly
5.4.8 **As who** as if he
5.4.11 **rid** get rid of

5.5
Sc. 18 *Enter Richard alone.*

RICHARD   I have been studying how I may compare
This prison where I live unto the world;
And for because the world is populous,
And here is not a creature but myself,
I cannot do it. Yet I'll hammer it out.   5
My brain I'll prove the female to my soul,
My soul the father, and these two beget
A generation of still-breeding thoughts;
And these same thoughts people this little world
In humours like the people of this world,   10
For no thought is contented. The better sort,
As thoughts of things divine, are intermixed
With scruples, and do set the word itself
Against the word, as thus: 'Come little ones',
And then again: 15
'It is as hard to come as for a camel
To thread the postern of a small needle's eye.'
Thoughts tending to ambition, they do plot
Unlikely wonders: how these vain weak nails
May tear a passage through the flinty ribs   20
Of this hard world, my ragged prison walls;

Sc. 18 5.5.1 **studying** meditating
5.5.3 **for because** because
5.5.6 **My...soul** (reverses the usual
stereotyping of reason as male, emotion
as female)
5.5.6 **the female** i.e. receptive
5.5.6 **soul** (here the source of emotions)
5.5.8 **still-breeding** ever-breeding
5.5.9 **this little world** i.e. the prison;
perhaps also Richard himself
5.5.10 **humours** temperaments; moods,
capriciousness (hence 'no thought is
contented')
5.5.10 **this world** i.e. the real world
5.5.12 **As** such as
5.5.12–13 **are...set** i.e. being intermixed
with scruples, set (in effect, the 'scruples'
themselves *set*)

5.5.13 **scruples** doubts, perplexities
5.5.14 **Come, little ones** (from Matthew
19:14, Mark 10:14, and Luke 18:25)
5.5.16–17 **It...eye** (misquotes Matthew
19:24, Mark 10:25, or Luke 18:25, which
speak of the unlikelihood of the rich
reaching heaven. Richard interpolates
'to come' and 'the postern'. The biblical
passages were interpreted as 'needle' as
the sewing implement, 'camel' as 'cable-
rope'; or 'needle' as 'small pedestrian
entrance in gateway to city walls', 'camel'
as the beast of burden. 'Postern' (small
back gateway) points to the latter.)
5.5.17 **needle's** (one syllable)
5.5.18 **Thoughts** i.e. other thoughts
5.5.19 **wonders** miracles
5.5.21 **ragged** rugged

And, for they cannot, die in their own pride.
Thoughts tending to content flatter themselves
That they are not the first of fortune's slaves,
Nor shall not be the last—like seely beggars,   25
Who, sitting in the stocks, refuge their shame
That many have and others must set there;
And in this thought they find a kind of ease,
Bearing their own misfortunes on the back
Of such as have before endured the like.   30
Thus play I in one person many people,
And none contented. Sometimes am I king;
Then treasons make me wish myself a beggar,
And so I am. Then crushing penury
Persuades me I was better when a king;   35
Then am I kinged again, and by and by,
Think that I am unkinged by Bolingbroke,
And straight am nothing. But whate'er I be,
Nor I, nor any man that but man is,
With nothing shall be pleased till he be eased   40
With being nothing.

   The music plays

                    Music do I hear.
Ha, ha; keep time! How sour sweet music is
When time is broke and no proportion kept.
So is it in the music of men's lives.
And here have I the daintiness of ear   45
To check time broke in a disordered string;

5.5.22 **for** because
5.5.22 **pride** arrogance; prime of life
5.5.23 **content** contentment
5.5.25 **Nor…last** i.e. not ever shall be
5.5.25 **seely** foolish, simple-minded
5.5.26 **refuge** find refuge for
5.5.27 **That** i.e. in the thought that
5.5.27 **set** be placed
5.5.38 **straight** at once
5.5.39 **but** merely
5.5.41.1 *music plays* (probably strings and/
   or wind instruments in early performances.
   The 1623 text cues the music one line

earlier, so that Richard clearly responds
to actual music, while the location of the
direction in the 1597 text can be staged so
that the audience understands the music
as an externalization of the music that
has been playing in Richard's mind. The
groom might play the music on stage, or
the music can be ethereal and with no clear
explanation of its source.)
5.5.43 **proportion** harmony
5.5.46 **check** rebuke
5.5.46 **disordered string** string
   instrument playing out of tune

But for the concord of my state and time
Had not an ear to hear my true time broke.
I wasted time, and now doth time waste me,
For now hath time made me his numb'ring clock.   50
My thoughts are minutes, and with sighs they jar
Their watches on unto mine eyes, the outward watch
Whereto my finger, like a dial's point,
Is pointing still, in cleansing them from tears.
Now, sir, the sound that tells what hour it is   55
Are clamorous groans which strike upon my heart,
Which is the bell. So sighs, and tears, and groans
Show minutes, times, and hours. But my time
Runs posting on in Bolingbroke's proud joy,
While I stand fooling here, his jack of the clock.   60
This music mads me. Let it sound no more,
For though it have holp mad men to their wits,
In me it seems it will make wise men mad.

    [*Music ceases*]

Yet blessing on his heart that gives it me,
For 'tis a sign of love, and love to Richard   65
Is a strange brooch in this all-hating world.

    Enter a Groom of the stable

GROOM   Hail, royal Prince!

RICHARD   Thanks, noble peer.
The cheapest of us is ten groats too dear.

5.5.47 **concord** harmony
5.5.47 **state** existence, condition
5.5.48 **Had not** i.e. I would not have had
5.5.50 **numb'ring clock** i.e. clock which counts the hours, as opposed to an hourglass
5.5.51–4 **My…tears** (The details of this conceit fit together imperfectly.)
5.5.52 **watches** clockwork mechanism
5.5.52 **outward watch** outer casing; outer sentry; hence the mind's outward watcher
5.5.53 **point** pointer, hand
5.5.54 **pointing still** always pointing
5.5.54 **cleansing them from tears** i.e. wiping tears from my eyes

5.5.55 **tells** count
5.5.58 **my time** i.e. the time appointed for my rule as king
5.5.60 **jack of the clock** (model human figure that strikes the bell of a clock on the hour or quarter-hour)
5.5.62 **holp** helped
5.5.66 **strange brooch** rare ornament
5.5.68 **The…dear** i.e. you have overpriced the cheaper of us in calling me 'royal'. This is a quibble on the coins called a 'royal' (worth 10 shillings), a 'noble' (worth 6 shillings), and a 'groat' (worth 4 pence). Ten groats is roughly the difference between the first two.
5.5.68 **cheapest** cheaper

What art thou, and how comest thou humbly hither,
Where no man never comes but that sad dog   70
That brings me food to make misfortune live?

GROOM   I was a poor groom of thy stable, King,
When thou wert king; who, travelling towards York,
With much ado at length have gotten leave
To look upon my sometimes royal master's face.   75
O, how it erned my heart when I beheld
In London streets, that coronation day,
When Bolingbroke rode on roan Barbary,
That horse that thou so often hast bestrid,
That horse that I so carefully have dressed!   80

RICHARD   Rode he on Barbary? Tell me, gentle friend,
How went he under him?

GROOM   So proudly as if he disdained the ground.

RICHARD   So proud that Bolingbroke was on his back.
That jade hath eat bread from my royal hand;   85
This hand hath made him proud with clapping him.
Would he not stumble, would he not fall down—
Since pride must have a fall—and break the neck
Of that proud man that did usurp his back?
Forgiveness, horse. Why do I rail on thee,   90
Since thou, created to be awed by man,
Wast born to bear? I was not made a horse,
And yet I bear a burden like an ass,
Spur-galled and tired by jauncing Bolingbroke.

   Enter [Keeper] to Richard with meat.

KEEPER [*to Groom*]   Fellow, give place. Here is no longer stay.   95
RICHARD [*to Groom*]   If thou love me, 'tis time thou wert away.

5.5.70 **sad** dismal-looking
5.5.75 **sometimes** formerly (qualifying 'royal'); or former (qualifying 'master')
5.5.76 **erned** grieved
5.5.78 **Barbary** (a favoured breed of horse; but here specifically the horse's name)
5.5.80 **dressed** groomed
5.5.81 **gentle** (a term of address usually reserved for the gentry)
5.5.85 **jade** (contemptuous term for a horse)

5.5.86 **clapping** patting
5.5.88 **pride...fall** (proverbial)
5.5.94 **Spur-galled** with sores caused by spurring
5.5.94 **jauncing** prancing. The image casts Bolingbroke as an exuberant rider of Richard, who does not share the horseman's enthusiasm.
5.5.95 **give place** leave

GROOM   What my tongue dares not, that my heart shall say.

Exit Groom

KEEPER   My lord, will't please you to fall to?

RICHARD   Taste of it first, as thou art wont to do.

KEEPER   My lord, I dare not. Sir Pierce of Exton,   100
Who lately came from the King, commands the contrary.

RICHARD   The devil take Henry of Lancaster and thee!
Patience is stale, and I am weary of it.

[*He strikes the Keeper*]

KEEPER   Help, help, help!

The murderers [Exton and his Men] rush in

RICHARD   How now! What means death in this rude assault?   105

[*He seizes a weapon from a man, and kills him*]

Villain, thy own hand yields thy death's instrument.
Go thou, and fill another room in hell.

Here Exton strikes him down.

RICHARD   That hand shall burn in never-quenching fire
That staggers thus my person. Exton, thy fierce hand
Hath with the King's blood stained the King's own land.   110
Mount, mount my soul; thy seat is up on high,
Whilst my gross flesh sinks downward here to die,

[*He dies*]

EXTON   As full of valour as of royal blood.
Both have I spilt. O, would the deed were good!
For now the devil that told me I did well,   115
Says that this deed is chronicled in hell.
This dead king to the living King I'll bear.
Take hence the rest, and give them burial here.

*Exeunt Exton with Richard's body at one door,
and his men with other bodies at the other door*

5.5.100 **I dare not** (A food-taster
originally tested for poison, but
tasting was more usually a courteous
formality. The keeper's instructions
not to taste are intended as an insult
to Richard.)

5.5.105 **What means death** what does
death mean by (but the exact sense is
uncertain)

5.5.109 **staggers...person** i.e. makes me
totter

5.5.111 **seat** resting-place

5.6

Sc. 19 [*Flourish.*] *Enter King Henry with the Duke of York*
         [*and other lords and attendants*]

KING HENRY   Kind uncle York, the latest news we hear
    Is that the rebels have consumed with fire
    Our town of Ci'cester in Gloucestershire;
    But whether they be ta'en or slain we hear not.

        Enter the Earl of Northumberland.

    Welcome, my lord. What is the news?   5

NORTHUMBERLAND   First to thy sacred state wish I all happiness.
    The next news is, I have to London sent
    The heads of Oxford, Salisbury, Blunt, and Kent.
    The manner of their taking may appear
    At large discoursèd in this paper here.   10

        [*He gives the paper to King Henry*]

KING HENRY   We thank thee, gentle Percy, for thy pains,
    And to thy worth will add right worthy gains.

        Enter Lord Fitzwalter

FITZWALTER   My lord, I have from Oxford sent to London
    The heads of Brocas and Sir Bennet Seely,
    Two of the dangerous consorted traitors   15
    That sought at Oxford thy dire overthrow.

KING HENRY   Thy pains, Fitzwalter, shall not be forgot.
    Right noble is thy merit, well I wot.

        [*Enter Harry Percy, with the Bishop of Carlisle, guarded*]

HARRY PERCY   The grand conspirator Abbot of Westminster,
    With clog of conscience and sour melancholy,   20
    Hath yielded up his body to the grave.
    But here is Carlisle living, to abide
    Thy kingly doom and sentence of his pride.

Sc. 19 5.6.3 **Ci'cester** Cirencester   5.6.10 **at large discoursèd** narrated in full
5.6.8 **Oxford** (The 1623 text rectifies a   5.6.12 **right worthy** very valuable; well-
    historical mistake by removing 'Oxford'   deserved
    (who was not part of the conspiracy) and   5.6.15 **consorted** confederated
    adding 'Spencer' between the other two   5.6.18 **wot** know
    names.)   5.6.20 **clog** burden

KING HENRY   Carlisle, this is your doom.
Choose out some secret place, some reverent room   25
More than thou hast, and with it joy thy life.
So as thou liv'st in peace, die free from strife.
For though mine enemy thou hast ever been,
High sparks of honour in thee have I seen.

Enter Exton with [his men bearing] the coffin

EXTON   Great King, within this coffin I present   30
Thy buried fear. Herein all breathless lies
The mightiest of thy greatest enemies,
Richard of Bordeaux, by me hither brought.

KING HENRY   Exton, I thank thee not, for thou hast wrought
A deed of slander with thy fatal hand   35
Upon my head and all this famous land.

EXTON   From your own mouth, my lord, did I this deed.

KING HENRY   They love not poison that do poison need;
Nor do I thee. Though I did wish him dead,
I hate the murderer, love him murderèd.   40
The guilt of conscience take thou for thy labour,
But neither my good word nor princely favour.
With Cain go wander through the shades of night,
And never show thy head by day nor light.

[Exeunt Exton and his men]

Lords, I protest my soul is full of woe   45
That blood should sprinkle me to make me grow.
Come mourn with me for what I do lament,
And put on sullen black incontinent.
I'll make a voyage to the Holy Land
To wash this blood off from my guilty hand.   50
March sadly after. Grace my mournings here
In weeping after this untimely bier.   *[Exeunt with the coffin]*

5.6.24 **doom** sentence
5.6.26 **More** i.e. more 'reverent'
5.6.26 **thou hast** i.e. the room thou hast
(a prison cell)
5.6.26 **joy** enjoy
5.6.35 **slander** disgrace

5.6.38 **They...need** (from proverbial 'to
love the treason and hate the traitor')
5.6.43 **With...night** Cain was condemned
to hide his face from God and be a
fugitive and a vagabond (Genesis 4:14).
5.6.48 **incontinent** immediately

American Literature

British and Irish Literature

Children's Literature

Classics and Ancient Literature

Colonial Literature

Eastern Literature

European Literature

Gothic Literature

History

Medieval Literature

Oxford English Drama

Philosophy

Poetry

Politics

Religion

The Oxford Shakespeare

A complete list of Oxford World's Classics, including Authors in Context, Oxford English Drama, and the Oxford Shakespeare, is available in the UK from the Marketing Services Department, Oxford University Press, Great Clarendon Street, Oxford OX2 6DP, or visit the website at www.oup.com/uk/worldsclassics.

In the USA, visit www.oup.com/us/owc for a complete title list.

Oxford World's Classics are available from all good bookshops.

	An Anthology of Elizabethan Prose Fiction
	Early Modern Women's Writing
	Three Early Modern Utopias (Utopia; New Atlantis; The Isle of Pines)
FRANCIS BACON	**Essays** **The Major Works**
APHRA BEHN	**Oroonoko and Other Writings** **The Rover and Other Plays**
JOHN BUNYAN	**Grace Abounding** **The Pilgrim's Progress**
JOHN DONNE	**The Major Works** **Selected Poetry**
JOHN FOXE	**Book of Martyrs**
BEN JONSON	**The Alchemist and Other Plays** **The Devil is an Ass and Other Plays** **Five Plays**
JOHN MILTON	**The Major Works** **Paradise Lost** **Selected Poetry**
EARL OF ROCHESTER	**Selected Poems**
SIR PHILIP SIDNEY	**The Old Arcadia** **The Major Works**
SIR PHILIP and MARY SIDNEY	**The Sidney Psalter**
IZAAK WALTON	**The Compleat Angler**

The Anglo-Saxon World

Beowulf

Lancelot of the Lake

The Paston Letters

Sir Gawain and the Green Knight

The Poetic Edda

The Mabinogion

Tales of the Elders of Ireland

York Mystery Plays

GEOFFREY CHAUCER   **The Canterbury Tales**
Troilus and Criseyde

GUILLAUME DE LORRIS   **The Romance of the Rose**
and JEAN DE MEUN

HENRY OF HUNTINGDON   **The History of the English People**
1000–1154

JOCELIN OF BRAKELOND   **Chronicle of the Abbey of Bury**
St Edmunds

WILLIAM LANGLAND   **Piers Plowman**

SIR JOHN MANDEVILLE   **The Book of Marvels and Travels**

SIR THOMAS MALORY   **Le Morte Darthur**

A SELECTION OF　　　**OXFORD WORLD'S CLASSICS**

CHARLES DICKENS	**The Old Curiosity Shop**
	Our Mutual Friend
	The Pickwick Papers
GEORGE DU MAURIER	**Trilby**
MARIA EDGEWORTH	**Castle Rackrent**
GEORGE ELIOT	**Daniel Deronda**
	The Lifted Veil and Brother Jacob
	Middlemarch
	The Mill on the Floss
	Silas Marner
EDWARD FITZGERALD	**The Rubáiyát of Omar Khayyám**
ELIZABETH GASKELL	**Cranford**
	The Life of Charlotte Brontë
	Mary Barton
	North and South
	Wives and Daughters
GEORGE GISSING	**New Grub Street**
	The Nether World
	The Odd Women
EDMUND GOSSE	**Father and Son**
THOMAS HARDY	**Far from the Madding Crowd**
	Jude the Obscure
	The Mayor of Casterbridge
	The Return of the Native
	Tess of the d'Urbervilles
	The Woodlanders
JAMES HOGG	**The Private Memoirs and Confessions of a Justified Sinner**
JOHN KEATS	**The Major Works**
	Selected Letters
CHARLES MATURIN	**Melmoth the Wanderer**
HENRY MAYHEW	**London Labour and the London Poor**